A Funny Kind of Day

A Farce

by John McIntyre

Evans Plays
London

Cast List

Tim Spring	Writer – Pleasant, cheerful, optimistic. 34yrs.
Katie Spring	His wife – Brisk, attractive personality. 31yrs.
Mrs –Er	Their daily – Vague and disapproving. 45 yrs.
Roger Weston-Lamb	Family friend – Smart but slightly stuffy. 35 yrs.
Boo-Boo	His girlfriend – Blonde, bosomy, brainless.28yrs.
Myrtle Boggsley	A guest – Eccentric, forceful. 42 yrs.
P.P. Taskley	American businessman – Genial but hardheaded. 50 yrs.

The play should be taken at a fast pace so that incredulity is suspended. Exits and the following entrances most of the time are instantaneous if not simultaneous.

Though Mrs –Er rarely completes a sentence the audience should always be aware of the word on her mind if not on her lips.

Time – The present. Summer.

Act I   Early Friday evening.

Act II   Ten minutes later.

The play was first presented at Church Hill Theatre, Edinburgh, by Edinburgh People's Theatre, on March 20, 1974, with the following cast:

TIM SPRING *S. SECOMBE* John Ramage
KATIE SPRING *R CORBETT* Judy Crighton
MRS -ER *KIN ROMBLE* Maureen Cochrane
ROGER WESTON-LAMB *T. ROMBES* Patrick Taylor
BOO-BOO *LEAH ROMBLE* Kati Reid
MYRTLE BOGGSLEY *LINDA BAKER* Cath Gourlay
P.P. TASKLEY *T LINEHAN* Alan Cochrane

Directed by John McIntyre

Set Design by Tom Bell

A FUNNY KIND OF DAY

The curtain opens on the living-room and garden of the SPRINGS' country cottage outside London. The garden occupies about a quarter of the
stage R. In it is seen the front of an old gypsy caravan, a bench and
some bushes. The front door of the cottage is in a back wall and a door
to the kitchen is D.L. with a service hatch just U.S. The right wall of the
cottage extends only halfway D.S. stopping at the french windows leading
to the garden. A staircase starts on the back wall then turns forward up
the left wall and leads to the bedrooms and bathroom. The space below
the stairs is occupied by a large cupboard,which houses the telephone and
has a window in the door. The room is furnished attractively with a desk,
settee and occasional chairs. There are various antique pieces around
the room,including an old gun on the wall.
Stereo turntable and loudspeakers are in evidence and there is a tiger-
skin rug on the floor.

It is early evening on a Friday. TIM is seated at desk,busily typing to
the closing strains of the William Tell Overture. He pauses, listening
to the music, and soon finds himself keeping time with a ruler. Warming
to the task,he arises to conduct the stereo speakers with considerable
energy. The piece is followed by tumultuous applause,which TIM ack-
nowledges with several deep bows, raising the imaginary orchestra to
its feet. He is engrossed in shaking hands with the non-existent leader
when the telephone rings. He has just taken it from the cupboard under
the stairs and answered it when the music starts again - this time bag-
pipes and drums.

TIM

Hello..... I'm sorry I can't quite ..... Hold on
a sec.... (He crosses to stereo controls, trips
over the head of the tigerskin.) That damn thing!
(Turns off stereo and returns to the telephone.)
Hello again. Tim Spring speaking..... Oh, it's
you, Mr Pritchard. We were just having a little
music..... Disturb my writing? No, not at all -
in fact it helps .... You don't think it helped the
August issue much? Ah well, I didn't have it then
you see. (Forces a laugh.) Now what was it you
.... September? It'll be on your desk first
thing on Monday morning. I'm putting the finishing touches on it now..... You think finishing
touches is a very appropriate way of putting it?..
.... Mr Pritchard, you can't possibly mean.....
You do..... I see .... You're working on the
circulation figures now...... I can't understand
it. Village Almanac is unique among women's
magazines .... I know it's old-fashioned,
that's why it sells - I mean that's why it should
sell. There's only Aunt Ada's Journal and that's
no competition...... You think it is I
promise you the September issue is fabulous ...
..... So was the unicorn and you don't see many
of them around. I take your point Mr Pritchard,
but surely you're not trying to tell me...... You
are.........I see. Well thanks for the gypsy's
warning anyway...... Bye.

(TIM puts telephone back in the cupboard and is
crossing the room dejectedly when he trips over
the tiger's head again.)

This thing has got to go.

(TIM picks up rug, growls at it and throws it in
the telephone cupboard.)

Hold that tiger!

(His own joke has cheered him up a bit and he
crosses to turn over the record. Reads off
record:)

'Sounds of the City'.

(TIM puts the record on and the sound of pneumatic drills fills the room. For a moment he
mimes the road-drilling, then seeing KATIE
coming up the garden, rushes back to his typing.
KATIE enters french windows with a basket con-
taining gardening implements and aerosol spray
and carrying a bunch of flowers. She speaks but
cannot be heard over the noise.)

KATIE   (Mouthing.) Will you turn that bloody thing down!

               (There is no response from TIM so she goes be-
               hind him and sprays him with the aerosol.)

TIM   What the ....? (He crosses to turn off the stereo
               and then sniffs himself.) What is that stuff?

KATIE   (Reading from can.) 'For all household pests.'
               I'd say that covered you.

TIM   It certainly has.

KATIE   Do you have to play that infernal machine so loudly?

TIM   I thought you might like to hear it down the garden.

KATIE   I go in the garden for bluebells not decibels. Tim,
               why did we come to live here in the wilds? Why
               did we leave the big city? Tell me again.

TIM   You know why - so I could get peace to write.

KATIE   Exactly. So we don't require any pneumatic drills.
               Why you bought the thing I'll never know. God
               knows we can't afford it. We've always got too
               much month left at the end of our money as it is.
               (Starts to arrange flowers.)

TIM   I thought you liked to listen to records.

KATIE   We've only got one record and that's the demon-

stration disc that came with it. We can't afford
to buy any more because your epic spy-thriller
'Thunderpussy' is only at chapter two and that
crummy rag you write single-handed only just pays
the rent.

TIM

(Annoyed) Rag? Rag? Village Almanac is very
good of its kind and it isn't everyone who is suf-
ficiently talented to be able to write in so many
different styles. It's very tiring having to be
Primrose Lane your homespun beauty columnist
on Mondays, Madge Playfair advice to the lovelorn
on Tuesdays and old Adam Sodworthy the gardener
on Wednesdays.

KATIE

Well, I wish old Adam would get in a bit more
practical experience. (Notices rug is missing.)
What have you done with our tiger rug?

TIM

I chucked it under the stairs. I'm fed up of trip-
ping over it.

KATIE

Me too. Still,it's a shame for it to be stuck in the
dark under there, when it would feel much more at
home in the jungle outside the window. Do you
know, even the weeds have greenfly. Why can't
we get a gardener in?

TIM

Because we can't afford it. Last month's money
went on the ster.... I mean I thought if you had a
little music you might enjoy your weeding more.
Don't you like the Dagenham Girl Pipers?

KATIE

Is that what it was?

TIM

They were beating retreat.

KATIE

I should advise you to do the same when you see
Mrs -Er. She hasn't been paid for two weeks.

TIM

Do we have to keep that woman? She never seems
to do anything more strenuous than plumping up
the cushions. Got an absolute mania for it.

KATIE   I meant to tell you. I found out about that.

TIM   You did?

KATIE   Seems her sister in London took her to the theatre
         - one of those drawing-room comedies. You know
         the sort of thing - curtain goes up and the house-
         keeper is found shaking up the cushions. The
         telephone rings, she answers it and gets the audi-
         ence up to date with the situation before the real
         plot starts.

TIM   And as that's her only function, the poor soul has
         nothing else to do but come on occasionally and
         beat up the bolsters. I know the sort of thing. A
         very hackneyed way of opening a play.

KATIE   Made a big impression anyhow. Now it's prac-
         tically her mission in life. She can hear kapok
         crumple at two hundred yards. Watch this.

         (KATIE disarranges a cushion. The kitchen door
         flies open instantly and MRS -ER enters, plumps
         up the cushion and replaces it.)

MRS -ER Have you finished with the -er? (She indicates the
         tea things on tray on desk.)

TIM   Not yet, Mrs -Er, I think I'll have another cup.
         (Helps himself to tea.)

MRS -ER (to KATIE.) The grocer was right out of -er, so I
         got a tin of -er instead. Will that be all right?

KATIE   Yes, of course, Mrs -Er.

MRS -ER Got to get on, then. Time and tide wait for no -er.
         (Exits to kitchen.)

TIM   One of these days she's going to finish a sentence.

KATIE   Funny though, you always know what she means.
         Another thing too, I find it's sort of -er.

TIM   Infectious. I know. Drives me up the wall. I
                           can't get any work done when she's around.

KATIE   Why don't you work in the caravan?

TIM   The caravan? Look at it. It's only the woodworm
                           holding hands that stops it from falling down. I
                           bet it's full of dead gypsies.

KATIE   Rubbish. It only needs a bit of a clean.

TIM   All right, I suppose I could give it a try. Get
                           Mrs -Er to give it a going over.

KATIE   Just at this moment I don't like to ask her. We
                           owe her two weeks' money, remember?

TIM   Can't you do it then?

KATIE   I have more than enough to do in the garden. You
                           want to work in the caravan - you clean it. It
                           can't be so bad. The people who had this cottage
                           before used to sleep in it.

TIM   We might be doing the same before long. Pritch-
                           ard was on the phone. Looks like Village Almanac
                           is on the skids.

KATIE   That's all we need.

TIM   He's going over the circulation figures now. If
                           things are as drastic as he thinks he'll stop pub-
                           lication at the end of the year.

KATIE   Does he really mean it?

TIM   He says he's thinking it over but I'm pretty sure
                           of the outcome.

KATIE   So it's curtains for Village Almanac.

TIM   Chintz ones I shouldn't wonder.

KATIE   That's the trouble. It's so dated. You'll have to
         change your image. All the old dears who buy it
         must be over seventy and there's fewer of them
         left every month. Extend your readership. Be a
         bit more with it.

TIM   That would just lose me the readers I've got. If I
         mentioned mascara my lot would think it was
         something for constipation.

KATIE   Well, you'll have to do something. I mean, look
         at this. (Picks up a copy of Village Almanac.)
         'Knit yourself a pair of cosy bedsocks'. That
         should go down well with the teeny-boppers. Where
         on earth did you get the pattern anyway?

TIM   It's the same one I always have. I just put down
         knit 1, slip 2, knit 2 together, purl 1, and so on
         till it covers the page. Looks exactly like the real
         thing and, let's face it, nobody will actually knit
         it.

KATIE   You hope.

TIM   Course they won't. It's already been a pair of
         mitts, an angora jumper and a set of egg cosies.
         Nobody's complained, which proves that nobody's
         tried to knit it. As a matter of fact,I make sure
         nobody tries the recipes either.

KATIE   How can you guarantee that?

TIM   I always put in something like one and a half pints
         of double cream,so people are terrified to try it
         because of the expense. Last month we had 'Stuf-
         fed Marrow with Sardine Cream Sauce'. Can you
         imagine anyone making that?

KATIE   Not twice. And certainly not your readers.

TIM   Of course not.They read Village Almanac because
         of the old-fashioned image. We've led them to
         believe that all the contributors like old Adam,

Madge Playfair, Sister Truscott on her faithful
bicycle and Deirdre Doubtfire and her crystal
ball all live here, next door to each other in a
beautiful Olde Englishe Village. It reminds them
of their youth. They're in the seventh heaven.

KATIE

Well you'll be in the first one if you don't get
September's copy off to Pritchard tonight.

TIM

Just got Deirdre's horoscopes to do. Still, I can
send them in later if I get this lot off. (Starts
putting typed pages in large envelope.) Do you
want to hear how the latest episode of the serial
ends?

KATIE

'Love at the Flower Show'? Not particularly.

TIM

Well, you remember how the new curate has fallen
in love with Violet Brown, the church organist?
One night after too much gooseberry wine at the
choir social he decides to declare his feelings,
and slips a poem he has written through her letter
box. Listen to this.

KATIE

I've never been less agog.

TIM

(Reading.) Just moments after meeting you I felt
                    that fate was kind,
I knew at once quite suddenly our hearts had inter-
                    twined.
For years I've searched for such as you with
                    whom to share my life,
My darling, how I love you - please consent to
                    be my wife.

KATIE

Yuch!

(TIM seals envelope, but has omitted poem which
is left on desk.)

TIM

Well it's a lot better than the rubbish they have in
Aunt Ada's Journal.

KATIE	Getting nasty about the opposition?
TIM	That's no competition. Stamps - where are they?
	(TIM searches through desk drawers as MRS -ER enters from kitchen.)
MRS -ER	You finished with the -er?
TIM	Yes, thank you, Mrs -Er. (TIM addresses and stamps envelope.)
MRS -ER	(Collecting tea things.) Butcher's sent you a nice piece of -er this week.
KATIE	Oh good.
MRS -ER	(to TIM) My late husband always liked his little bit of -er on a Sunday morning.
TIM	Don't we all.
KATIE	Tim!
MRS -ER	Now before I go there's just the little matter of my -er.
TIM	Her -er?
KATIE	Mrs -Er's -er.
TIM	Oh, her -er.
KATIE	I'm sorry, Mrs -Er, but we forgot to go to the bank today.
MRS -ER	I see.
TIM	As a matter of fact, Mrs -Er, we're a bit short of the ready till the end of the month. Could you possibly, I mean could you wait till then?
KATIE	I'm afraid we've had rather a lot of expenses

	recently.
MRS -ER	Well I'm sure you didn't need to buy that there -er.
KATIE	(With an icy look at TIM.) For once I entirely agree with you.
TIM	But Mrs -Er, I don't think you realise how much pleasure you'll get out of it all as well.
KATIE	Yes. If the excitement isn't too much for her she can listen to the Dagenham Girl Pipers while she's punching the cushions.
TIM	Honestly, you'll love it. (TIM manoevres MRS -ER to a spot between the two speakers.) Stand there to get the full effect. (Consults record.) Side two - animal noises. Listen to this. (The room is filled with the sound of roaring jungle beasts. MRS -ER remains impassive.) What do you think of that?
MRS -ER	Very nice I'm sure, but I'd rather have had my -er.
TIM	I'm sorry if you think it was an extravagance.
MRS -ER	My late husband always used to say you should cut your -er according to your -er.
TIM	I'm afraid we haven't any cloth to cut at all. And no way of getting any till the end of the month.
MRS -ER	What about B and B?
TIM	B and B?
MRS -ER	Bed and -er.
KATIE	Bed and breakfasts. We've got a spare room. Why not?
TIM	I am not having strangers living in my house.

MRS -ER   My neighbour did all right when that there pop
                 festival was on. She had Dirty Dave and the Arm-
                 pits for bed and -er.

TIM   Who?

KATIE   Dirty Dave and the Armpits. They're a pop group.

TIM   (angry) You expect me to open my house to people
                 like that? To have them sleeping in my beds and
                 using my bathroom? I might stretch a point if it
                 was Julie Andrews, but I don't like the thought of
                 Dirty Dave squeezing his spots at my mirror and
                 using my loo.

MRS -ER   Why don't you give it a -er?

TIM   Mrs -Er you have said quite enough. It's out of
                 the question.

MRS -ER   All right then, I'm going. I shall finish today but
                 if you want me back after that I shall require to
                 see the colour of your -er.

                 (MRS -ER picks up tea things and exits to kitchen.)

KATIE   Tim, don't you think we could....

TIM   I thought I made it perfectly clear I want no one
                 staying in my house. There's just one week to
                 work on 'Thunderpussy' before I have to start on
                 October's Village Almanac. At one week a month
                 it'll take five years to finish. (Shouting.) I want
                 peace and quiet! Now, those bloody horoscopes.

                 (TIM takes down vase containing dozens of slips
                 of paper with typed forecasts on them and proceeds
                 to draw from it as in a raffle.)

KATIE   But we need the money. I've never known any-
                 body so pig-headed. Roger warned me you were
                 stubborn.

TIM

Dear Roger. My boyhood buddy and your ex-boy-friend. (Draws a slip of paper.)

KATIE

Don't sneer. He's done very well for himself. And he's very understanding.

TIM

He's very clever too. He never got married. (Reads.) 'Capricorn. Family matters go well. Do not get over-tired midweek. Lucky colour - blue. ' (Types.)

KATIE

Well, whoever gets him will be damned lucky. He asked me you know.

TIM

He was drunk that night. The same as I was when I proposed.

KATIE

If you'd gone into the yoghourt business with him we'd have been rolling in it.

TIM

I have no desire to roll in yoghourt. (Picks out another paper.) Sagittarius.

KATIE

And when I think how smart he always looks - shoes polished, not a speck of dandruff.

TIM

When he dyes his hair the dandruff gets dyed as well. That's why you don't notice it. (Reads.) 'Travel plans favoured this month. Make new friends. Romance is in the air. Lucky colour - puce. '

KATIE

You forgot my birthday last month, he didn't. He's so thoughtful - look at what he sent me.

TIM

I don't have to look. I can smell it.

KATIE

He knew I'd be pleased with a ton of manure for the garden. You will spread it for me?

TIM

Certainly not. It can lie there till it rots.

KATIE

Oh, it has rotted. It's ready to spread now.

TIM   Definitely not. That's exactly what he intended to
                       happen. One of his more ingenious practical jokes.
                       Well, I'm not falling into it.

KATIE   I'm not asking you to fall into it, just spread it.

TIM   It's a mystery to me what women see in him. I
                       mean, look at that gorgeous bird he's got in tow at
                       the moment. What a cracker!

KATIE   How do you .... ? Oh yes, that party in town at
                       the Whittaker's you went to on your own when I
                       was visiting mother. What's her name again?

TIM   Everyone calls her Boo-Boo.

KATIE   Whatever for?

TIM   Because she's got the most gorgeous pair of -er
                       eyes, blonde hair and an uncomplicated mind.

KATIE   I heard she didn't have any mind at all. Don't
                       think I like the sound of her. Let's hope he
                       doesn't bring her when he comes down for the...

TIM   The what?

KATIE   (weakly) The weekend. It's just that I happened
                       to run into Roger last week in town and said that
                       if he..... if ever he..... just to let us know.

TIM   (In a rage.) Let me tell you straight that if ever
                       I come in here and find Roger in this house I shall
                       walk straight out and never come back, and when
                       I do he'd better be gone. This isn't a weekend
                       retreat, it's where I work - preferably without
                       interruption. I want no bed and breakfasts and
                       definitely no Roger Weston-Lambs. Is that clear?
                       (Looks at watch.) Damn, I'll miss the post.

                       (TIM stamps out of the front door with the enve-
                       lope. KATIE, annoyed, throws a cushion after
                       him. Instantly MRS -ER enters from kitchen,

picks it up and replaces it.)

KATIE   What am I going to do, Mrs -Er? About Roger,
                   I mean?

MRS -ER   Beg your -er?

KATIE   Roger, that is, a friend of ours, phoned this after-
                   noon to say he's coming for the weekend. I haven't
                   got around to telling Tim. He'll be furious.

MRS -ER   That's not my -er, I'm sure. I've got another
                   half-hour to go to finish my week and that's the
                   last you'll see of me unless I get my -er. (Exits
                   to kitchen.)

KATIE   But Mrs -Er, I'm sure we can ... (Telephone
                   rings.) Ellersley 225...... I'm sorry, Mr Spring
                   isn't at home ..... Oh, you actually wanted to
                   speak to Deirdre Doubtfire? Well, I'm afraid she
                   doesn't exactly live here.......Yes, I do know
                   her..... Very well indeed...... A personal
                   horoscope? No, I don't think ..... Could you call
                   this afternoon?...... Well, perhaps if you could
                   telephone again in a few minutes my husband
                   should be back...... Whom shall I say? ....
                   Mr Taskley..... I'll tell him.... Goodbye.
                   (KATIE closes cupboard door and turns to desk to
                   make a note. She picks up a piece of paper with
                   poem on it.)   Oh no, he's forgotten to put that
                   puke-making poem in.

                   (As she re-reads it ROGER enters through french
                   windows, steals across and puts his arms round
                   her.)

                   Roger!

ROGER   Hello, darling. (Kisses her.)

KATIE   Roger, for heaven's sake!

ROGER   What's the matter?

KATIE   Tim'll be back any minute.

ROGER   Good. How is he? Thought I'd never get here.
The old bus packed up just before the village. One
of the local yokels directed me across the fields.

KATIE   Then he hasn't seen you?

ROGER   You mean it'll be a surprise for him?

KATIE   It certainly will.

ROGER   It's great to have friends like you and Tim, and to
be able to come down to the country for a bit of
peace and quiet. (Flops into chair.) Could I
trouble you for a duster, my shoes seem to have
got a bit messed up.

                              (KATIE exits to kitchen returning immediately
with a box of cleaning materials as ROGER con-
tinues:)

                              My love life hasn't been going too smoothly and I
need time to sort things out. (Takes duster.)
Thank you. (Wipes shoes.) Oh no, I seem to
have pulled a thread on my sleeve. I paid a hundred and forty guineas for this.

KATIE   Yoghourt must be doing well.

ROGER   Just like having your own private mint. Mint!
I've just thought of a new flavour. I must write
that down. (Does so.)

KATIE   Roger, you can't stay. Tim's very busy this
weekend and can't be distracted by having any-
body here.

ROGER   (Unheeding.) As I was saying things haven't been
going too smoothly. It's Boo-Boo. I forgot you
haven't met her, but Tim has. Anyway, I think
this is it. She's gorgeous.... I've always been
crazy about blondes and she's got the most beaut-

iful pair of -er eyes you've ever seen.

KATIE   I'm very pleased for you but what I was trying to..

ROGER   The trouble is that everywhere we go she just
               mesmerises all the men. Any party you go to
               she's got a crowd round her. I say she encourages
               them. We have arguments all the time. You
               can't imagine what it's like having arguments all
               the time.

KATIE   I think I can.

ROGER   I was going to bring her down for the weekend, but
               she turned up at a party last night in a dress that
               was so tight she looked like a melon smuggler.
               In ten seconds she had every man in the room
               round her. I mean I'm glad she has a good figure
               but the trouble is that all the women start getting
               antagonistic towards me for bringing her. I didn't
               enjoy myself a bit so I got mad and walked out and
               left her there.

KATIE   We've all got our problems. Mine is how to get
               you out of this house without offending you. I'll
               give you one drink before you go.

ROGER   I'll have a gin. What do you mean, before I go?

               (KATIE pours a gin for ROGER.)

KATIE   I explained but you weren't listening. Tim's in
               one of his creative moods and can't be disturbed.
               I'm sorry. Please go back to London.

ROGER   But I don't want to see Boo-Boo till I've had time
               to think things out. Besides, the car won't go.

KATIE   Roger, it's impossible.

ROGER   There must be somewhere I can put my head down.

KATIE   Well, I suppose there is the caravan.

ROGER   That sounds more like it.

KATIE   Only as a last resort. Try your very best to get
someone in the village to fix the car, but if the
worst comes to the worst I imagine you could
sleep out there and leave first thing in the morning
before Tim sees you. He really would go berserk.

ROGER   O.K., but I think you're exaggerating.

KATIE   I promise you I'm not. It's this new book he's
writing. The characters seem to be taking him
over - it's all tearing black silk, mouthfuls of
smashed teeth and kicks in the groin.

ROGER   His Mickey Spillane period? All right, I'll be
discreet.

KATIE   Fine. On your way, then.

ROGER   When I've finished my drink.

KATIE   Now!

        (KATIE takes ROGER's glass and pushes him out
of the french windows. She has just closed it and
turned when TIM enters the front door.)

TIM   Bit early for you to start drinking. (Sniffs half-
full glass in KATIE's hand.) Gin? You never
drink gin.

KATIE   I was going to clean my engagement ring. (Drops
ring in gin.)

TIM   There's enough for the crown jewels in there.

KATIE   It's all right, I won't waste it. (She downs the
contents of the glass and then retrieves the ring
from her mouth and puts it on.)

TIM   You seem a bit on edge.

KATIE	Do I? Yes, I suppose I am. Had this phone call when you were out - a Mr Taskley. Sounds like an American. He wants to meet Deirdre Doubtfire.
TIM	Whatever for?
KATIE	Something about a personal horoscope.
TIM	A nut case. I hope you told him there was nothing doing.
KATIE	He was very persuasive. He's phoning again.
TIM	That's all we need.
	(KATIE picks up cleaning things.)
	Where are you going with these?
KATIE	(airily) I thought I'd give the caravan a clean after all.
TIM	But you said.....
KATIE	I know and I'm sorry, darling. It won't take long.
	(KATIE exits through french windows and enters caravan. TIM takes paper from vase.)
TIM	Leo. A busy month ahead. Try to.... (Doorbell rings. TIM answers it and BOO-BOO is seen.)
BOO-BOO	Is Roger Weston-Lamb here?
TIM	Boo-Boo!
BOO-BOO	(Entering.) Tim! Thank goodness I've found the right place. Where's Roger?
TIM	I don't know. Where's he supposed to be?
BOO-BOO	I thought he was coming here for the weekend.

TIM	Over my dead .... I mean no.
BOO-BOO	Oh dear!
TIM	How did you get here?
BOO-BOO	I got a lift from a friend. She dropped me with my cases at the end of the road. Perhaps Roger will be here soon.
TIM	Not so far as I know.
BOO-BOO	(In tears.) What am I going to do? We had a dreadful row last night and I wanted to make up.
TIM	(Offering handkerchief.) Would this be any help?
BOO-BOO	He says it's all my fault. He says I wear my clothes too tight. I can't help it - they just don't make things big enough. You see my problem.
TIM	(Ogling.) I'm just turning it over in my mind.
BOO-BOO	And now he's gone off and I don't know where and I can't get back to London and I wish I was dead. (Sobs.)
TIM	(Putting an arm around BOO-BOO.) Please don't cry. You can stay the night here and go back to London in the morning.
BOO-BOO	Wouldn't your wife mind? Most of Roger's friends' wives don't like me very much. I don't want to cause any trouble. You're sure she wouldn't mind?
TIM	Well, not exactly positive. She likes Roger so she'd probably take his part.
BOO-BOO	Nobody's ever on my side. (More tears.) I'd better go.
TIM	There must be something I can do... Wait a minute ......Yes!

BOO-BOO   You mean I can stay?

TIM   Yes, you can stay.

BOO-BOO   You're so sweet. (Throws herself at TIM and
               kisses him.)

TIM   I know you're only showing your gratitude but
               please don't do that.

BOO-BOO   You don't like being kissed? I kiss everybody all
               the time.

TIM   Well, if you want to stay you'd better miss me out.

BOO-BOO   I'm sorry. Please can I stay?

TIM   Yes, but I think it would be better if Katie didn't
               know who you are. We've been considering taking
               people in for bed and breakfast, so you can be the
               first.

BOO-BOO   Super. What do I do?

TIM   Go away and come back in about twenty minutes
               and ask if we have a room.

BOO-BOO   Come back in twenty minutes and ask for bed and
               breakfast. I've got it.

TIM   That's right. Pretend you're a total stranger.

BOO-BOO   Thank you, Tim. You're so sweet. (She kisses
               TIM and exits through front door.)

TIM   (Calling after her.) You're not supposed to know
               me.

               (TIM removes calendar from wall, writes BED
               AND BREAKFAST on it in felt pen and lays it on
               desk. KATIE leaves caravan with cleaning mat-
               erials and enters cottage, while TIM busies him-
               self with horoscopes.)

Leo. A busy month ahead. (Types.)

KATIE	It wasn't as bad as I thought it might be.
TIM	Good. I'll go in there and finish the horoscopes.
KATIE	I wouldn't do that just now. I have the blankets airing.
TIM	I'm not going to sleep there.
KATIE	Of course not, silly. It's just that they needed doing.
TIM	I'll go straight in there tomorrow and get cracking on 'Thunderpussy'. Thanks for cleaning it, anyway.
KATIE	I was a bit hasty before. I'm sorry.
TIM	I wasn't very nice before either when we were talking about bed and breakfasts. I think it's a super idea.
KATIE	You do really?
TIM	Yes, I do. It might be quite interesting meeting different people, you know - strangers.
KATIE	That's true. It might even help you with your book. When do we start?
TIM	Right away. (Shows her the notice.) Look I've made a notice. If it's a success I'll make a wooden one later, but this'll do to hang on the gate tonight. (Exits through front door.)
KATIE	(Calling.) Mrs -Er. (There is no response so KATIE disarranges a cushion and MRS -ER appears instantly from the kitchen.) I wanted to tell you that Tim has reconsidered. We're going in for bed and breakfasts after all. (MRS -ER looks disinterested; plumps cushion.) I knew you'd be

pleased.

MRS -ER   Just let me know when you've made the money to
                          cover my -er.

KATIE   Do you suppose I could ask them to use the outside
                          loo at the bottom of the garden?

MRS -ER   If you do you'll get mud tramped right through the
                          -er.

KATIE   I forgot. There's that great muddy puddle in front
                          of it. It must be about six inches deep.

MRS -ER   Not to mention that heap of steaming -er beside it.

KATIE   Yes, that's not a very good idea. (Picks up
                          cleaning materials.) Still, I'm glad Tim's enthu-
                          siastic. We should cope very well.

MRS -ER   I hope so, because I won't be here to help to -er.

                          (KATIE exits to kitchen with cleaning materials.
                          MRS -ER gives the cushions a going-over.)

TIM   (Entering front door.) Hello, Mrs -Er.

                          (She pauses.)

                          Carry on punching. Well, we're open for bed and
                          breakfasts. What do you think of that?

                          (No response.)

                          I knew you'd be pleased. Shouldn't have long to
                          wait, the roads are quite busy.

MRS -ER   Just so long as I get my -er.

                          (Telephone rings. TIM answers it on the threshold
                          of the cupboard. MRS -ER punches cushions.)

TIM   Ellersley 225....... Tim Spring speaking......

Yes, my wife told me you had called..... You
want a personal astrolger? Well, I'm Miss
Doubtfire's editor, but I don't think she would....
Not even for how much?...... How much?......
Well, perhaps she might consider it....... Tell
me more........

(Door bell rings. MRS -ER opens it and MYRTLE
is seen outside.)

MRS -ER   Yes?

MYRTLE   I saw your notice and wondered if I could have
               accommodation for   tonight?

MRS -ER   I'll see. (Crosses to TIM.)

TIM   Why yes, Mr Taskley. I'll think of something -
               I mean I'm sure she'd consider it........ You'd
               like to come round now?

MRS -ER   There's a woman here wants bed and -er.

TIM   (To MRS -ER without looking round.) Yes, that's
               fine. (To telephone.) I'm sure she'd be most
               suitable.

MRS -ER   (Crossing to MYRTLE.) Mr Spring says you'll
               be most suitable.

MYRTLE   Jolly good! Could you possibly give me a hand
               with my luggage? (Exits.)

MRS -ER   (Following her off.) It's not my job to carry
               people's -er.

TIM   You're at the crossroads? Well, take the second
               on the ..... Oh, I see - the crossroads in your
               life. But where are you geographically?.......
               Uh-huh.... Carry on to the village, then, and it's
               about two miles after that. There's a side road
               on the left...... A proposition to put to me as
               editor as well?....... Yes, I might be interested.

.......Fine....... Look forward to meeting you.
Bye, Mr Taskley.

(KATIE enters from kitchen.)

KATIE   Was that the bell?

TIM   Never mind that just now. That was Taskley on
                the phone.

KATIE   Your star-struck nut? Still wants a personal
                astrologer, does he?

TIM   My star-struck, gold-plated nut. He says all the
                big businessmen in the States have astrologers
                and he's offering Deirdre 10,000 dollars a year.

KATIE   But there is no Deirdre.

TIM   He doesn't need to know that. I'll just cable the
                forecasts over.

KATIE   Nobody's going to pay you 10,000 dollars for a one-
                man raffle.

TIM   I suppose you're right. Still, perhaps I can find a
                more traditional way of doing it. Let's think. What
                did they do in the past?

KATIE   The ancient Roman soothsayers used entrails.

TIM   Ugh!

KATIE   I don't know. If you used liver and kidney we
                could have it for lunch when you had finished with
                it.

TIM   For heaven's sake be serious. This is important.

KATIE   He's sure to want to meet Deirdre personally.

TIM   We'll cross that bridge when we come to it. Any-
                way I'd better do a bit of astrological reading-up.

There's a book in the bedroom. (TIM makes for stairs.) Bedroom! That reminds me, our first bed and breakfast has arrived. (Exits upstairs.)

KATIE   We certainly didn't have to wait long.

(MYRTLE and MRS -ER enter with luggage.)

MYRTLE   How do you do?

KATIE   How do you do? I'm Mrs Spring. Mrs -Er would you take -er ...

MYRTLE   Miss Boggsley.

KATIE   Miss Boggsley's things upstairs?

(MRS -ER exits upstairs with cases, muttering.)

MYRTLE   (Effusively.) What a beautiful cottage, Mrs Spring. Such atmosphere.

KATIE   Why, thank you. I hope you'll be comfortable. If there's anything you would like don't hesitate to ask.

MYRTLE   I do confess to being rather peckish. Could you possibly manage a crumb?

(MRS -ER comes downstairs.)

KATIE   Certainly. Mrs -Er could you - I mean would you .... a sandwich, do you think?

(MRS-ER walks on unheeding into kitchen.)

She'd love to make you one.

MYRTLE   How kind. I really only intended staying one night, but I feel so much at home. The vibrations ......

KATIE   It's only the heavy lorries on the main road. They won't disturb you.

MYRTLE   The spiritual vibrations. I'm very sensitive to such things. You see, it's an auspicious time for me - with

the moon in the fourth house and my birth sign in
trine with Venus and Mercury.

KATIE   Pardon?

MYRTLE   The stars herald my personal nirvana. (KATIE
still looks puzzled.) A man is about to enter my
life. Do you believe in astrology?

KATIE   Well, I....... (Picks up horoscope vase to re-
place it.)

MYRTLE   Do you hold the key to the future in your hands?

KATIE   (Looking at vase.) I suppose you could put it like
that. I think I've got the key. It's the lock I'm
looking for. (Replaces vase.)

MYRTLE   There should be a constant search for a deeper
understanding of the occult.

KATIE   That's exactly what my husband's doing upstairs
right now.

MYTLE   A kindred spirit - how fortuitous. Perhaps he
can help me.

KATIE   Oh, he just dabbles. It's much more likely that
you can help him.

MYRTLE   I'm sure I could on the mathematical side. I've
always been hot on maths.

KATIE   Oh good.

MYRTLE   It's the heiroglyphics I have trouble with. How are
his pentacles?

KATIE   All right the last time I looked.

MYRTLE   I'm sure we'll get on splendidly. When we know
each other better perhaps he'll let me take a peek.

KATIE	Who can tell? Well now, shall I show you to your room?
MYRTLE	Not at all, just tell me where it is.
KATIE	First door at the top of the stairs and the bathroom is at the end of the passage.
MYRTLE	(Making for stairs.) If I get lost I can always fall back on my divining rod.
KATIE	Watch out for splinters.
MYRTLE	I'll just have a wash,then come down for my fodder and we can have a good chinwag. (MYRTLE exits upstairs.)
KATIE	(Calling.) Mrs -Er.
	(There is no reply so KATIE crosses to hatch and tries to peer through crack between doors. She puts her ear to the crack to listen, the doors fly open and MRS -ER's face appears.)
MRS -ER	Yes?
	(KATIE recoils.)
KATIE	Oh! I asked you to rustle up a sandwich for Miss Boggsley but I couldn't hear you rustling.
MRS -ER	And what am I supposed to put in this here -er?
KATIE	Anything you like. Isn't there any -er?
MRS -ER	It's finished. I suppose I'll have to open a jar of -er.
KATIE	No, I think a tin of -er. There's one in the top cupboard.
MRS -ER	(Slamming doors.) Extravagance.

(TIM comes downstairs with books.)

TIM   Should be something in this lot.

KATIE   Our B and B seems to be very pleasant.

TIM   Oh good, you've met her. Not really my type -
a bit flash and brainless.

KATIE   I wouldn't call her that. Apparently she's quite
a mathematician.

TIM   Mathematician?

KATIE   She has to be for her astrological work. Could be
quite a help to you I should think. (TIM looks
puzzled.) I'd better go and chivvy Mrs -Er. It
seems our guest is starving.

     (KATIE exits to kitchen. BOO-BOO enters front
door and comes close to TIM before speaking.)

BOO-BOO   Well, I'm here.

     (TIM jumps.)

TIM   You're here. Yes. It all seems to have gone
quite smoothly.

BOO-BOO   If we're going to do it properly I'm going to have
to pay tomorrow and I don't know if I have enough
money. I thought I had only 75 pence with me but
I found another 44 so that's... (calculates on her
fingers) ...£1.85.

TIM   You're quite a mathematician.

BOO-BOO   Will that be enough? (Kisses TIM.)

TIM   Quite enough. I've told you. Don't do that.

BOO-BOO   I love your cottage. I'm so glad I came. My
horoscope said to stay at home this weekend, but

I don't believe in any of that old rubbish.

(Sandwich on a plate is pushed through hatch by MRS -ER.)

A sandwich. Good. I'm starving. (Starts to eat sandwich.)

TIM   I'm glad something seems to be true.

BOO-BOO   My cases are still down at the main road. Will you help me?

TIM   Yes, of course.

BOO-BOO   I'll carry the little one with my make-up but I can't manage the other and you look so strong.

TIM   (pleased) Well, that's what men are for.

BOO-BOO   So they are. I don't believe in Women's Lib at all. Besides, Roger says if I burned my bra it would take three fire engines to put out the blaze.

(BOO-BOO and TIM exit front door. MYRTLE comes down stairs, makes sure she is alone and snoops furtively round the room going through desk drawers and papers. KATIE's entrance from kitchen startles her.)

KATIE   I hope your room is satisfactory, Miss Boggsley.

MYRTLE   Do please call me Myrtle. Yes, my room's just what the doctor ordered - a lovely Wedgwood.

KATIE   Pardon?

MYRTLE   The walls - the colour of the walls. I've been suffering from blue starvation, you see.

KATIE   Wasn't your sandwich all right?

MYRTLE   I'm afraid I haven't been offered one yet.

KATIE

I'm sorry. It's all ready. (Picks up empty plate.) Oh! I do apologise. My husband must have eaten it. I'll see about another.

MYRTLE

Well, if you wouldn't mind. I am rather peckish.

KATIE

It's no trouble. (Opens hatch.) Mrs -Er, I wonder if we could have another sandwich.

(MRS -ER glowers through hatch and slams doors.)

She says she'll be delighted.

MYRTLE

How kind. No, Mrs Spring, when I spoke of blue starvation I was not referring to my digestive processes. I have the stomach of an ostrich.

KATIE

Good gracious.

MYRTLE

I meant my aura was a bit off-colour - over-saturated with red, I think. The blue of the bedroom will cool it down.

KATIE

I'm so glad, Miss Boggsley.

MYRTLE

Myrtle.

KATIE

Yes, of course. Myrtle. And you must call me Katie. May I take your coat?

MYRTLE

Good heavens, I meant to leave it upstairs.

(MYRTLE removes coat which KATIE hangs over chair. She is wearing a skirt and a very odd jumper with an extra sleeve emerging from the bust line.)

I see you're admiring my outfit.

KATIE

It's very unusual.

MYRTLE

I knitted it myself and I think I made a slight mistake with the pattern. It seems to have this extra

	sleeve, but I just drape it round like this, (demonstrates) do you see. I've overheard lots of comments about it.
KATIE	It would certainly stand out in a crowd.
MYRTLE	If you'd like to knit one I can lend you the pattern. It was in Village Almanac.
KATIE	I should have guessed.
MYRTLE	What a wonderful little magazine. Their recipes are fabulous. Have you tried 'Stuffed Marrow with Sardine Cream Sauce'? I have it at least twice a week.
KATIE	I don't believe it.
MYRTLE	And the 'Tripe and Gooseberry Mousse' just melts in the mouth. It's a teensy bit extravagant with $1\frac{1}{2}$ pints of cream in it, but perfect for a special occasion.
KATIE	My husband, Tim, would be pleased to hear how enthusiastic you are about Village Almanac.
MYRTLE	Oh?
KATIE	He's the editor, you see.
MYRTLE	Of course! Spring. Russell Spring!
KATIE	Don't let him hear you call him that. He's rather embarrassed about being called Russell Spring - it was his mother's favourite piano solo at the time he was born.
MYRTLE	Good job it wasn't Rose Marie.
KATIE	You're right there. Anyway, he prefers Tim, his second name.
MYRTLE	How exciting to think that I'm staying in the very

countryside where 'Village Almanac' has its roots.
I only got off the bus here on an impulse. Per-
haps I shall be able to meet Madge Playfair,
Primrose Lane and all the other writers.

KATIE   We don't usually see much of them at weekends.

MYRTLE   (Crossing to french windows.) What a quaint old
                  caravan..... Wherever did you get it?

KATIE   It came with the house. It seems it is your gen-
                  uine old horse-drawn gypsy model.

MYRTLE   Romany lore has always fascinated me. Do you
                  think I could possibly take a peek inside?

KATIE   It's in a bit of a mess, but help yourself.

MYRTLE   Thank you.

KATIE   When you come back your sandwich should be
                  ready.

MYRTLE   How kind. (Exits through french windows.) I'm
                  off with the raggle-taggle gypsies - oh! (Enters
                  caravan.)

                  (MRS -ER enters from kitchen with sandwich on
                  plate.)

MRS -ER   Here's your -er.

KATIE   Thank you, Mrs -Er.

MRS -ER   And may I say that bed and -er does not include
                  providing -er every five minutes of the -er.

KATIE   I'll bear it in mind, Mrs-Er.

                  (MRS -ER exits to kitchen,muttering.
                  ROGER comes up garden and taps at french
                  window.)

Oh no, don't tell me...

(Crosses to window, with sandwich, and opens it.
ROGER enters.)

ROGER   Sorry, old love, they can't fix it - at least not
               until tomorrow. Looks like I'm staying. Good
               girl - a sandwich. (Takes sandwich.)

KATIE   Roger, no.

               (ROGER takes a bite.)

               Too late.

ROGER   Don't want to get you into trouble so I'll just nip
               into the caravan before your lord and master
               appears. (Makes to exit.)

KATIE   You can't. There's somebody in there.

ROGER   I know, your lover. You might have given me
               first refusal.

KATIE   Roger, for heaven's sake, there isn't much time.
               Now, where can you hide? I know - the outside
               loo at the bottom of the garden.

ROGER   This is ridiculous. I can't believe Tim hates me
               as much as that.

KATIE   You do have a reputation with married women,
               and he's very jealous. In his present state of
               mind he'd probably take a potshot at you. Roger,
               please go and hide. (Points.) To the loo!

ROGER   Toodeloo!

               (ROGER exits down garden as TIM enters front
               door with large suitcase.)

KATIE   More luggage? We'll never get it all in the room.

TIM   Eh? There's just another small case but our
               guest's right behind me carrying it herself.

KATIE   You're mistaken. She's in the caravan.

TIM   I tell you, she's bringing up the rear.

KATIE   Hang about. (Calls through french windows.)
               Miss Boggsley!

TIM   Who?

MYRTLE   (Opening top half of caravan door.) Hello!

TIM   My God!

               (BOO-BOO appears at the front door carrying a
               small case. TIM slams the door in her face.)

KATIE   Do come and meet my husband.

MYRTLE   Love to. (She leaves caravan and enters french
               windows.)

KATIE   (To TIM.) I don't know how you haven't met, but
               this is our guest.   Miss Boggsley, this is my
               husband, Tim.

MYRTLE   How do you do? I think you were telephoning when
               I arrived.

TIM   Yes, yes I was. (to himself) I must have got my
               lines crossed.

KATIE   Well, that's settled that. By the way, you ate
               Miss Boggsley's sandwich.

TIM   I did? I mean, I did. I'm so sorry, I'll get you
               another.

               (TIM picks up cushion and shakes it like a bell.
               MRS -ER enters instantly from kitchen.)

Could we have another sandwich, please?

MRS -ER	She's had two already.
TIM	Mrs -Er!
MRS -ER	I haven't got three pairs of -er. I'm not a horse.
TIM	What can a horse possibly have three pairs of? Wait a minute, she says she made two sandwiches. If I ate one, then who.....?
KATIE	I forgot, I ate the other. I do apologise. Would you mind Mrs -Er?

(MRS -ER exits to kitchen, muttering.)

MYRTLE	What a beautiful caravan - such atmosphere, most relaxing. Do you think I could sleep there instead of in the cottage?
KATIE	Well, I.....
MYRTLE	Oh, please. I'd love to sleep in the caravan with the browns.
TIM	The Browns? Are they staying here too?
MYRTLE	You misunderstand. You see my aura is rather red.....
TIM	I hope it's not infectious.
KATIE	Tim!
MYRTLE	...... and I thought I needed a touch of the blues........
TIM	I'm sorry, we don't have any Ella Fitzgerald records.
MYRTLE	...... but it's the browns that I need.

TIM	Well, Ella Fitzgerald's brown. But we only have the one record, you see.
MYRTLE	Pardon?
KATIE	This is getting quite beyond me.
MYRTLE	I'd so love to sleep alfresco.
TIM	Wear what you like.
MYRTLE	So please may I sleep in the caravan?
TIM	Certainly.
KATIE	I'm afraid not.
TIM	Why ever not? Why can't she sleep in the caravan? There's nobody sleeping there - apart from the Browns, apparently. Is there?
KATIE	Er, no. Of course not.
TIM	Good, that's settled, then.
MYRTLE	Thank you so much.
KATIE	(resignedly) I suppose I'd better see to the bed-clothes. They're airing.
MYRTLE	I'll give you a hand.
	(KATIE and MYRTLE exit through french windows.)
KATIE	I'm afraid you won't be very comfortable. Are you sure?
MYRTLE	I shall be perfectly all right. It's kind of you to take so much trouble.
	(KATIE and MYRTLE enter caravan. BOO-BOO enters front door with a small case which she puts down. TIM sees her.)

TIM	Boo-Boo, you can't stay.
BOO-BOO	Can't stay? But you said......
TIM	I know, but circumstances have changed. We're full up. No more bed and breakfasts.
BOO-BOO	You said you had a vacancy.
TIM	I had. Right between my ears.
BOO-BOO	But where can I sleep?
TIM	In your own bed. You'll have to go back to London.
BOO-BOO	But if Roger comes I'll miss him. I must see Roger.
TIM	If Roger comes I'll send him right back. You'll have to go - I have a very important business meeting.
BOO-BOO	You're not being very nice to me.
TIM	What time is it? (Looks at watch.) There's a bus at the end of the road in ten minutes. (TIM grabs large case.)
BOO-BOO	And I used to think you were sweet.
TIM	(Taking BOO-BOO's arm.) Come on!
	(A sandwich appears through the hatch.)
BOO-BOO	Can I have that sandwich?
TIM	Anything, but please hurry.
	(BOO-BOO takes sandwich and TIM bundles her through the front door, with large case, as KATIE and MYRTLE leave caravan and enter french windows.)

MYRTLE   It really is peaceful here. No sense of rush or bustle.

KATIE   Yes, it's very quiet here.

MYRTLE   The only sound seems to be my tummy rumbling. Do you suppose......?

KATIE   Yes, of course. Your snack should be ready now. (Crosses to hatch and sees empty plate.) Oh!

MYRTLE   What's the matter?

KATIE   I'm afraid your sandwich seems to have gone again.

MYRTLE   A poltergeist, do you suppose?

KATIE   If that's what I married, yes. I do apologise. I'll go and see about another.

MYRTLE   I'm sorry to be so much trouble, but I am growing weaker every minute.

KATIE   In two minutes there will be another sandwich, I promise.

MYRTLE   I'll just go and get my things from upstairs, then, and put them in the caravan.

                        (MYRTLE exits upstairs. KATIE opens the hatch revealing MRS -ER's furious face.)

KATIE   Oh!

MRS -ER   Was there something?

KATIE   Let me think. Yes, I'm sure there was. Miss Boggsley is enjoying your sandwiches.

MRS -ER   Oh yes.

KATIE   I wonder if you could possibly manage another.

MRS -ER	There isn't any more -er. She'll have to make do with -er.
	(Hatch doors slam shut. ROGER comes in from garden and taps on french windows. KATIE lets him in.)
ROGER	That place is filthy. Can I get in the caravan now?
KATIE	Sorry, you'll have to stay where you are.
ROGER	No. It's full of cobwebs and earwigs and beetles.
KATIE	(Giving him aerosol spray.) Try some of that.
ROGER	And the stench. It's right next to a ruddy great manure heap.
KATIE	Roger, I forgot. (Kisses him.) Thank you very much.
ROGER	What's that for?
KATIE	The manure. It was exactly what I wanted.
ROGER	I wish I'd sent you a book token. It's very draughty out there. Why can't I go in the caravan?
KATIE	I'm afraid someone else is going to sleep there.
ROGER	Then where the hell am I going to sleep?
KATIE	You'll have to sleep in the spare room now.
ROGER	(Making for the stairs.) Well, that's an improvement.
KATIE	You can't go up yet. Miss Boggsley's in the spare room.
ROGER	Who in heaven's name is Miss Boggsley?
KATIE	Never mind. Go back to the outside loo, and

when the coast's clear I'll ring this bell. (demonstrates) When you hear it don't waste any time.
Rush straight up the garden and into the first room
at the top of the stairs. Got it?

ROGER   O.K. if that's the only way. When I hear the bell,
run up the garden and straight upstairs.

(A sandwich on a plate is pushed through hatch.)

Good girl, you've got me another sandwich. Any
chance of some coffee?

KATIE   Roger, I can't let you have that sandwich. It's
for Miss Boggsley.

ROGER   Everything seems to be for Miss Boggsley. Why
can't I have it?

KATIE   Roger, please go and hide in the loo again.

ROGER   I refuse.

KATIE   Please. Just for me.

ROGER   Well, all right - if I can have that sandwich.

KATIE   No you can't.

ROGER   Not going then.

KATIE   O.K. you win. There you are. (Passes sandwich.) Now will you go!

ROGER   I'll have to hold my nose while I eat it.

(Exits through french windows and disappears
down garden as MYRTLE comes downstairs with
luggage.)

MYRTLE   (Seeing KATIE holding plate.) How kind. I see
you have my . . . . Oh!

KATIE   Oh dear. What must you think of me?

MYRTLE   I'm sure you're not doing it on purpose. It just
               seems like it. I think I shall faint in a minute.

KATIE   (Calling.) Mrs -Er.

               (No response. KATIE disarranges a cushion and
               MRS -ER in outdoor clothes appears instantly
               from kitchen.)

MRS -ER   Don't tell me, I can guess. Her eyes must be
               bigger than her -er. There's very little bread
               left, and that's for my blackbirds. I'm off now.
               Let me know when you've got my -er, and if it
               isn't within the next twenty-four hours you can
               take your job and -er. (Exits to kitchen.)

KATIE   I've never heard such language.

MYRTLE   Oh dear, I'm sorry if it's my fault. She does
               seem rather brittle, though. Has all the bread
               gone?

KATIE   I'm sure the blackbirds won't mind sharing. I'll
               see to it myself. Let me help you with your cases
               first.

MYRTLE   I think you'll have to. I'm too weak to carry them
               myself.

               (KATIE and MYRTLE exit french windows with
               cases.)

               I shouldn't really have brought so many clothes
               but I didn't know how long my little tour was going
               to be, and I like to be prepared for all weathers.
               I'll change before I have my fodder, then go for
               a stroll.

KATIE   I promise I'll have something waiting.

               (KATIE and MYRTLE enter caravan.)

MYRTLE   (Enthusiasm wearing a bit thin.) How kind.

                (TIM and BOO-BOO enter front door.)

TIM   Trust you to leave something behind. (TIM picks
                up BOO-BOO's small case.) The bus passes in
                three minutes exactly and it's the last one today.

BOO-BOO   You're not being very nice to me and if that's your
                attitude I'll carry it myself. (Tries to take case
                from TIM.)

TIM   Don't be silly. I'll take it.

BOO-BOO   (Struggling.) Let go. I'll manage.

                (The case bursts open, spilling an assortment of
                make-up on the floor.)

TIM   Now look what you've done.

                (TIM and BOO-BOO get down on the floor to pick
                up the make-up. KATIE leaves caravan and enters
                by french windows. TIM sees her and starts to
                take an exaggerated interest in the case contents.)

                That's very nice. I'm sure Katie would like that.
                (Dabs perfume on wrist and sniffs.) Citrus with
                musky undertones, would you say?

BOO-BOO   Pardon?

TIM   (Trying lipstick shades on hand.) What a beaut-
                iful colour! This really is a convenient way to
                buy presents. I'd been wondering what to get for
                my wife's birthday, then I heard your ding-dongs.

BOO-BOO   My ding-dongs?

TIM   You know. Ding-dong, Hathaway-calling!

BOO-BOO   Hathaway?

TIM   (Making a big thing of seeing KATIE.) Katie!
                        Well, well, well. You've burst in on my little
                        secret.

KATIE   I'm not surprised you've kept her a secret.

TIM   Don't be silly. This charming young lady is our
                        local Hathaway Cosmetics representative. I was
                        just doing a little ordering. (to BOO-BOO) Oh,
                        sorry, Miss -er, this is my wife.

BOO-BOO   (effusively) Hello.

KATIE   (drily) Good afternoon.

TIM   Could I have two jars of that, a tube of that and a
                        half pint bottle of that.

BOO-BOO   Thank you very much, sir.

KATIE   (to TIM) May I ask what you're going to use for
                        money?

BOO-BOO   Oh dear, I've missed my bus.

TIM   Oh dear, she's missed her bus.

BOO-BOO   What am I going to do now?

TIM   What is she going to do now?

BOO-BOO   Is there any place round here where I could stay
                        the night?

TIM   Is there any place round here where she could....
                        Wait a minute. She could stay here.

KATIE   We charge six pounds for bed and breakfast if
                        there's no advance booking.

BOO-BOO   Six pounds?

TIM   Six pounds!

KATIE   Plus V.A.T.

TIM   Hang about. How much do the things I ordered
                come to?

BOO-BOO   Six pounds.

TIM   Plus V.A.T. Isn't that a coincidence.

KATIE   Yes, isn't it.

TIM   That's settled, then. You stay here tonight and
                we don't owe each other anything.

BOO-BOO   Super. Thank you very much.

TIM   (Ushering BOO-BOO to front door.) I'm sure
                you'll have some other calls to make in the
                village, so we'll see you later. It's been a
                pleasure doing business with you. Goodbye.

BOO-BOO   Goodbye. I mean ding-dong. (Exits.)

KATIE   That was a bit silly. You know we've only got
                one spare room.

TIM   But Miss Boggsley's sleeping in the caravan, so
                it's still vacant.

KATIE   Is it?

TIM   Of course it is. What's the matter? Can you
                think of any reason why we can't let it?

KATIE   No, I suppose not.

TIM   That's it all sorted out then. As a matter of
                interest, what's Myrtle doing now?

KATIE   She's in the caravan changing, then she's going
                for a walk. That reminds me - I said I'd have
                some food ready for her. (Crosses to kitchen
                door.) Oh, I meant to tell you, you've left out

the last page of the serial from the stuff you sent
to Pritchard. Better get it off tonight. (Exits.)

(TIM crosses to desk and re-reads poem.)

TIM
Just moments after meeting you I felt that fate
                                    was kind,
I knew at once quite suddenly our hearts had
                                        intertwined.
For years I've searched for such as you with whom
                                to share my life,
My darling, how I love you - consent to be my
                                        wife.

(TIM sniffs perfume on his wrist and makes a face.
He puts poem in envelope as the doorbell rings.
Leaving envelope on desk, he answers door.
TASKLEY is seen outside.)

TASKLEY
Hi there!

TIM
You must be Mr Taskley. Do come in.

(TASKLEY enters.)

TASKLEY
Happy to make your acquaintance, Russell.

TIM
My friends call me Tim.

TASKLEY
Then I'll call you Tim. Sorry to give you such
short notice of my visit, but this is the way I do
business. Spur of the moment, you know.

TIM
That's quite all right.

TASKLEY
Haven't much time as I'm leaving for the States
first thing in the morning, so I'll lay it on the
line for you.

TIM
Please do.

TASKLEY
Fact is I happened on a copy of Village Almanac
somebody left in a railway carriage - first class

of course - and I was very impressed by your
astrology page.

TIM   I'm so glad.

TASKLEY   That Deirdre Doubtfire sure is a shrewd cookie.
               I followed the advice she gave under my sign.
               'Buy your fruit this week,' she said. So I did.

TIM   You make jam?

TASKLEY   I made jam all right. Cabled my broker and
               bought shares in South Seas Pineapple. On Tues-
               day of this week they were taken over by Hawaiian
               Amalgamated and I made fifty thousand dollars on
               the deal. That's cool, isn't it.

TIM   Tooth-chattering.

TASKLEY   That's why I want Deirdre as my personal astro-
               loger. Half the corporations in the States have
               them, and I used to pooh-pooh the idea - but not
               now. No sir, not now. You think she'd sign up
               with me?

TIM   Well, I.....

TASKLEY   I need her assistance right now. I have a prob-
               lem, you see. I want to know whether I'd be
               better with magazines or paper tissues.

TIM   I suppose it depends what you want them for.
               Tissues are great if you have a cold, but there's
               not much reading on them. I've never heard of
               anyone curling up with a good tissue.

TASKLEY   You misunderstand me. At this moment in time
               my company produces both tissues and magazines,
               but it isn't economic to diversify and I want to
               switch entirely to whichever has the better pros-
               pects. You've heard of Taskley's Tinted Tissues,
               of course?

TIM	Not recently.
TASKLEY	No? They come in lemon, peach, lime and orange.
TIM	Is that the colour or the flavour?
TASKLEY	Trouble is, tissues are getting saturated.
TIM	Isn't that what they're for?
TASKLEY	The market is saturated. You can't make people use any more. Average consumption is 6.83 tissues a day.
TIM	6.83? I sometimes have trouble getting them out of the box in one piece myself.
TASKLEY	For a decent profit margin I have to increase that to at least 10.2 a day. The question is how?
TIM	I don't know. Unless there's a way of increasing the pollen count.
	(KATIE enters from kitchen with a sandwich on a plate.)
	Mr Taskley, I'd like you to meet my wife, Katie. Katie, this is Mr Taskley.
KATIE	How do you do, Mr Taskley?
TASKLEY	Happy to make your acquaintance, Katie. But please, all my friends call me P.P.
TIM	Mr Taskley, I mean P.P., is very anxious to meet Deirdre.
KATIE	(Under her breath.) So am I.
TASKLEY	(Looking round.) You have a beautiful home, Katie. I do so admire all your little antique items.
KATIE	There's really nothing of value except that gun on

<table>
<tbody>
<tr><td></td><td>the wall there. It still works, you know, and we keep it loaded, but don't worry - we haven't shot any visitors for months.</td></tr>
<tr><td>TASKLEY</td><td>Now you're teasing. Say, that's a most attractive little object.</td></tr>
<tr><td>TIM</td><td>Just an old cow bell, that's all. (Passes it to TASKLEY.)</td></tr>
<tr><td>TASKLEY</td><td>A cow bell? Imagine! (Rings bell.) The sound of these must carry quite a long way.</td></tr>
<tr><td>TIM</td><td>Yes. You can hear it right at the bottom of the garden.</td></tr>
<tr><td>KATIE</td><td>Mr Taskley, I wonder if you'd mind not.....</td></tr>
<tr><td></td><td>(TASKLEY rings bell loudly. Shouts and oaths from ROGER offstage, then he rushes up garden wet and dripping. He enters french windows and falls flat on his face.)</td></tr>
<tr><td></td><td>..... Sodworthy, how dare you come bursting into the house like that.</td></tr>
<tr><td>ROGER</td><td>(Unrecognisable with muddy face.) It was your bloody idea.</td></tr>
<tr><td>KATIE</td><td>That's what I was trying to explain, Mr Taskley. We use that bell when we want to summon the gardener.</td></tr>
<tr><td>TIM</td><td>The what?</td></tr>
<tr><td>KATIE</td><td>Mr Taskley, may I introduce Adam Sodworthy.</td></tr>
<tr><td>ROGER</td><td>What did you call me?</td></tr>
<tr><td>KATIE</td><td>He's very good at his job though he looks so decrepit.</td></tr>
<tr><td>ROGER</td><td>Now see here, this has gone.......</td></tr>
</tbody>
</table>

KATIE	I tell my friends Tim won't let me have anybody more presentable in case I have an affair like Lady Chatterley, in which case Tim would get his shotgun out. We often laugh about it, don't we, Adam?
ROGER	(Catching on.) Aaarr! (From now on ROGER uses rustic voice.)
TASKLEY	Of course. Adam Sodworthy. I read your last month's column on the vegetable garden in Village Almanac. I'm very pleased to meet you.
	(Shakes hands with ROGER and gets mud on his hands.)
ROGER	Thank 'ee kindly, sir.
TASKLEY	Do you have a favourite vegetable yourself, Adam?
ROGER	I always say there's nothing like a nice early pea.
KATIE	I thought you might say something like that. Hadn't you better be getting back to what you were doing Adam?
ROGER	Aaarr! They mangel-wurzels be wantin' mulchin'. Good arternoon, zur. Arternoon, master. Thank 'ee kindly, ma'am.
	(ROGER bows himself out of french windows, dropping handkerchief.)
TASKLEY	A real son of the soil, eh?
TIM	A real son of a something. (to KATIE) Who the hell......?
TASKLEY	Could I use your smallest room, I wonder?
TIM	Smallest room? The telephone's right over there.
TASKLEY	(Indicating dirt from ROGER'S handshake.) I mean I seem to have got myself a little mussed.
KATIE	Certainly, Mr Taskley. The bathroom's at the

end of the passage upstairs.

TASKLEY   Thanks, Katie. Excuse me. (Exits upstairs.)

KATIE   Well, don't keep me in suspense.

TIM   That's just what I might do - by your thumbs. Who
                   was that walking compost heap?

KATIE   Do you think Taskley will swallow your horoscopes?
                   Is there some money in it?

TIM   Looks like there'd better be if you're employing
                   gardeners all over the place. Who is he? Where
                   did he come from? I don't care, get rid of him.
                   Yes, I do care. Who is he?

KATIE   Just a man who came to the door. I felt sorry for
                   him. Asked if we had any odd jobs.

TIM   Seemed very well-dressed for an odd-job man.
                   (Picks up handkerchief.) Has his handkerchief
                   monogrammed, I see. R.W. hyphen L. Roger
                   Weston-bloody-Lamb! I thought I told you.....

KATIE   Tim, you can't send him away. He just happened
                   to be passing and his car broke down.

TIM   How very convenient. And you employed him as a
                   gardener?

KATIE   You know I didn't. I thought it would impress
                   Taskley.

TIM   I don't want him here.

KATIE   He can't go back to London in case he bumps into
                   Boo-Boo.

TIM   Should be a soft landing. (Remembers.) Boo-Boo!
                   He definitely can't stay.

KATIE   You must admit he's been some help. He added
                   local colour for Taskley. Let him stay.

TIM	The answer is no. I'm not going to argue any more.
TASKLEY	(Entering from upstairs.) What a character that Sodworthy is. America is going to be crazy about him.
TIM	America is?
TASKLEY	Sure. I'd better explain. Taskley Incorporated publish two periodicals. One of them, 'Homespun', is similar to your 'Village Almanac' only it's sheer hokum dreamed up by a bunch of guys in the city who wouldn't know which part of a cow to pull to get service.
TIM	How deceitful.
TASKLEY	Exactly. Sales are dropping because the insincerity is showing through, and there I think you can help me.
TIM	Anything at all, P.P.
TASKLEY	My plan is this. I want to meet all your writers - those wonderful rustic characters who all live and work right here in this village - and if they fit in with my picture of them, as old Adam did, then I'll sign them up and Village Almanac can syndicate their columns to us for a substantial sum.
KATIE	How substantial?
TASKLEY	If you pay peanuts you get monkeys. How does twenty thousand dollars an issue grab you?
TIM	Very gently. I'll get in touch with our contributors right away.
TASKLEY	I've got some back numbers in the car you might like to take a look at. Excuse me.
TIM	I'd like to see them very much, Mr Taskley.

TASKLEY	P. P.
TIM	I think I'd rather call you Mr Taskley again.
	(TASKLEY exits front door.)
KATIE	(Flinging her arms round TIM.) We're going to be rich!
TIM	You want a gardener? I'll get you Percy Thrower. But what are we going to do? How can we swing it?
KATIE	Well, we've got Roger for a start. He can stay now?
TIM	I insist. Adam Sodworthy must stay, and we'll try to rustle up a few more tomorrow.
KATIE	Hang on. I can see old Adam coming up the path now. Disappear. I'll fix it.
TIM	Good girl.
	(TIM exits to kitchen. KATIE opens french windows for ROGER, who has by now cleaned himself up.)
ROGER	What made you ring that bloody bell? I thought you said......
KATIE	I didn't ring it, Roger, but that was certainly quick thinking on your part, pretending to be the gardener.
ROGER	On my part?
KATIE	Only you've gone and got cleaned up. Wait a sec. (She gets potted plant from window-sill.) Hold that.
	(ROGER holds plant pot and KATIE starts to dirty his face with earth.)
ROGER	Just a minute. What is this?

KATIE	It's a pelargonium.
ROGER	I mean what are you trying to do?
KATIE	Make you look more like a gardener, of course. Keep still.
ROGER	That went in my mouth.
KATIE	Won't make you talk any dirtier than usual. (Surveys her work.) Not bad, but you don't smell like a gardener.
	(KATIE exits to kitchen. ROGER looks at his tie and takes it off to make sure it has not been soiled. KATIE enters with a string of onions.)
	Good, you've taken your tie off. (She hangs string of onions round ROGER's neck. Sniffs.) That's much better.
ROGER	Look here, I've no intention of.....
KATIE	(Interrupting)...... being shot. I'm glad you've realised I wasn't exaggerating.
ROGER	Wouldn't it be simpler if I just told Tim the car had packed up and.....
KATIE	No, Roger. Not after all the deceit you've been practising. Tim would never forgive you. And he'd be bound to smell a rat if the new gardener suddenly disappeared. He'd make enquiries in the village and find out there was no such person. He'd think I'd been having an affair. Please stay, for my sake, Roger. Please, just until tomorrow, then we'll let him sack you.
ROGER	I've never been sacked in my life. I'll hand in my notice, like a gentleman.
KATIE	Whatever you say, only promise you'll act like a gardener till tomorrow.

ROGER   I suppose anything's better than sleeping under a
               hedge.

KATIE   Good. (Looks at him.) You still look too tidy.
               (Gets string from desk.) You could tie up your
               trouser legs with that. Now off you go and start
               living the part.

               (KATIE bundles ROGER out of french windows.)

ROGER   I'm not going back to that septic tank.

KATIE   Use the potting shed, then. There's a pair of
               boots and an old hat in there you could wear.

               (KATIE bundles ROGER out and he disappears
               down garden.)

               All clear, Tim!

               (TIM enters from kitchen, laughing.)

TIM   I think I'm going to enjoy having Roger Weston-
               Lamb as my gardener.

KATIE   Poor Roger. He did look so miserable.

               (They laugh. TASKLEY enters front door with
               magazines.)

               Oh, hello, Mr Taskley. Are these your magazines?

TASKLEY   I'm afraid I can only show you one of them, Katie.
               The other is strictly stag. There you are. (Gives
               magazine to KATIE.) 'Homespun' - the country-
               folk magazine. (Gives TIM the other one.) Can't
               show this to the little wife - eh, Tim?

TIM   'Fleshpot'.

TASKLEY   Catchy, uh?

TIM   You throw it and I'll catch it. (Looks at magazine.)

Gosh. Wow! (Opens centre-fold picture.) You
must use very strong staples.

KATIE
(Looking at 'Homespun'.) Very attractive, P.P.
How's the circulation?

TIM
Pounding!

KATIE
Tim Spring, you put that down before you burn
your fingers.

TASKLEY
(to TIM) I don't really have a lot to do with
'Fleshpot', but if I see an attractive girl on my
travels I do try to persuade her to pose for our
centre spread.

KATIE
(Glancing over their shoulders.) And the girls
accept?

TASKLEY
There is a financial inducement. Well now, when
am I going to meet Miss Doubtfire, Sister Truscott
and the rest?

TIM
Yes, well -er. A meeting? You want to meet
them. Of course. Yes.

KATIE
Tomorrow. We'll ask them to tea tomorrow.

TASKLEY
Tea? Tomorrow? I'm afraid that's no use. I
have to be back in London tonight and I take off
for the States in the morning at eight hundred
hours.

TIM
But you must stay.

KATIE
Yes, of course you must.

TASKLEY
Can't be done. If I can't meet the folks just now
we'll have to forget about the whole proposition.
It's all here in Deirdre Doubtfire's column. I
have the clipping here. (Produces clipping from
wallet and reads:) 'Friday is the only safe day
for major decisions.' If that woman made me

fifty grand on pineapple I can't afford to ignore the rest of her forecast.

KATIE (to TIM) Now I know what hoist with your own petard means.

TASKLEY The folks all live right here in the village. Why can't you phone them and have them stop round now?

TIM They've..... They've all gone off on a coach tour.

TASKLEY Where to?

TIM It's a mystery tour.

TASKLEY What time do they get back?

TIM That's the mystery.

KATIE Can't you stay just a little longer. (Sudden inspiration.) Have a sandwich.(Passes plate to him.)

TASKLEY (Taking sandwich.) I don't want a sandwich. I have to leave.

TIM Would you like to talk to old Adam again?

TASKLEY No thanks. I guess we'll just have to forget about the whole idea.

(TIM pacing across to window, sees MYRTLE emerge from the caravan wearing a leopard pattern coat. She hold out hand to check for rain and re-enters caravan. TIM has a sudden idea. TASKLEY is shaking hands with KATIE.)

Well, goodbye, Katie. It's been so nice visiting with you. I hope some day we might meet again.

KATIE I hope so too. If you're ever over here on business again......

TIM   (Looking at watch.) Good heavens, it's seven o'-
                        clock. (Urgently.) It's seven o'clock, Katie.

KATIE   (Not comprehending, but playing along.) Good
                        heavens, yes. So it is!

TIM   I'm afraid you can't leave now, Mr Taskley.
                        Nobody is allowed to go through the Safari Park
                        after seven o'clock.

TASKLEY   Safari Park?

TIM   Didn't you notice all the animals on the way here?

TASKLEY   I did see a cow.

TIM   No cows here. It must have been a water buffalo.
                        You see,this cottage is right in the middle of a
                        Safari Park full of leopards and things. (He
                        motions to KATIE to join in.)

KATIE   Yes - leopards and lions and tigers and... and...
                        walruses.

TIM   Steady on.

TASKLEY   But why can't I leave?

TIM   At seven o'clock all the animals are rounded up
                        into an enclosure at one end of the park for the
                        night. It so happens this cottage is right in the
                        middle of it. If you left now you wouldn't even
                        reach your car. (Glancing through window.) I
                        think that was one of the lions passing.

KATIE   Good old Simba!

TASKLEY   (Crossing to window.) Where? Where? I didn't
                        see.....

TIM   (Snatching TASKLEY's spectacles from his nose.)
                        No wonder. Your glasses need cleaning.(Passes
                        spectacles to KATIE.) Katie, take Mr Taskley

into the kitchen and clean his glasses so he can
see the wildlife.

TASKLEY

Hey, I'm almost blind without them.

KATIE

(Guiding TASKLEY towards kitchen.) This way,
Mr Taskley. You must see Simba.

(MYRTLE emerges from caravan, having added a
hat to her leopard ensemble. Made of the same
material as the coat, its shape incorporates cat-
like ears and two large red stones glow like eyes.)

TIM

Try to hurry. I don't want you to miss Spotty the
leopard. She's in the back garden.

(KATIE pushes TASKLEY, still holding sandwich,
into kitchen. MYRTLE enters french windows.)

MYRTLE

I'm just off for my constitutional, but if I don't
get something to eat first I won't have the strength
to go. My stomach is growling.

TIM

(Under his breath.) Good. Keep it going.

MYRTLE

Pardon?

TIM

Miss Boggsley, what a truly stunning outfit.

MYRTLE

Do you like it? How kind.

TIM

And those beads. So unusual. (Looking at beads
closely.) Whatever are they made of?

MYRTLE

Plastic, I think.

TIM

They're very pretty. (He breaks string of beads,
which scatter all over floor.) How clumsy of me.
I'm so sorry.

(MYRTLE gets down on hands and knees and
disappears behind a piece of furniture, picking
up beads. TIM moves smartly to the record

turntable and switches on sound of roaring beasts
at full volume. He then picks up chair and stands
with it like an animal trainer. TASKLEY rushes
in from kitchen followed by KATIE holding his
glasses. MYRTLE, on all fours, appears from behind furniture and approaches TASKLEY. She sees
his sandwich and leaps at it.)

MYRTLE   Food!

(TASKLEY falls in a dead faint. MYRTLE grabs
the sandwich and wolfs it down.)

Curtain

ACT II

Ten minutes later.

The tiger-skin rug is in a life-like position over a bench in the garden, facing the caravan. KATIE is seated and TIM is pouring two drinks. He takes one to KATIE.

TIM   Here, sink this. We've got some quick thinking
                           to do.

                           (TIM returns to drinks tray and picks up an empty
                           glass. Pacing up and down he takes a drink from
                           it, realises it is empty, changes it for the full one
                           and resumes his wanderings.)

KATIE   For God's sake stop pacing up and down like that.

TIM   What do you expect me to do? How you can
                           calmly sit there doing nothing with so much at
                           stake......

KATIE   I'm not doing nothing. I'm biting my nails.

TIM   Then bite them faster. We have the goose that
                           lays the golden eggs out cold in the caravan but
                           one false move and they're scrambled.

KATIE   He's not going to be very happy when he wakes up.
                           Do you think he'll make a scene and insist on
                           leaving?

TIM   Who knows? Anyway, it doesn't make much
                           difference unless we can come up with something.
                           He wants to meet my non-existent staff, remem-
                           ber?

KATIE	Well, he thinks he's met Adam Sodworthy already, though I don't know how long Roger will play up. You'd better go out and threaten him a bit.
TIM	And what the hell can we do about Deirdre Doubt-fire? He's bound to want to meet her. I mean, she's the whole reason for his being here.
KATIE	I don't know. Isn't it desperate, just when the future looks brighter......
TIM	Fate kicks you in the crystals.
KATIE	That's it! Myrtle!
TIM	Myrtle?
KATIE	Myrtle can be Deirdre.
TIM	But he's seen her.
KATIE	Only as leopard-woman. She's just the sort of eccentric he'd expect, and she's mad keen on astrology.
TIM	It might work. But what about the rest? I mean, there's Primrose Lane the Beauty Editor......
	(Doorbell rings.)
KATIE	Ding-dong. That's the answer.
TIM	Ding-dong?
KATIE	The broad of Avon.
TIM	Oh hell, I'd forgotten she was coming back.
KATIE	Pardon?
TIM	I mean yes, what a super idea.
KATIE	Do you think we could ask her to do it?

TIM   We don't ask her - we just introduce her. She's
               so dim she wouldn't realise. I can handle her.

KATIE   I hope that won't be necessary.

               (Doorbell rings again.)

               Well, don't just stand there, let her in.

               (TIM opens front door and BOO-BOO enters with
               small case.)

TIM   Hello, there.

BOO-BOO   I hope I haven't come back too soon. I don't want
               to be any trouble. I'll just go straight up if you'll
               show me my room.

KATIE   Nonsense, it's far too early. Come and sit down.
               We're so cut off from civilisation here we do enjoy
               the company of our visitors.

BOO-BOO   Well......

TIM   I can see why you're a beauty counsellor. Isn't
               she gorgeous, Katie?

KATIE   Tell me your secret.

BOO-BOO   My secret? Well, I came here looking for Ro....

TIM   (Interrupting.) The secret of your lovely hair.
               It's just the colour of -er.....

KATIE   Straw?

TIM   Primroses. Yes - primroses. I don't know
               what your name is, but I'm going to call you
               Primrose.

KATIE   Primrose. What an unusual name. I bet your
               surname is attractive too. Don't tell me. Let's
               see if I can guess.

TIM	I know who you remind me of. Did you see that musical at Drury .... Drury....
BOO-BOO	Lane?
KATIE	Pardon?
BOO-BOO	Lane.
KATIE	Lane - no I'd never have guessed that, but it is a pretty name. Primrose Lane.
TIM	Primrose, Katie was a little shy about asking, but since you're staying here she wondered if you could be prevailed upon to demonstrate your con- siderable talents in beauty culture.
BOO-BOO	Well, I'm not really very......
KATIE	Good. That's extremely kind of you. Tim, isn't that kind of Primrose?
TIM	Yes, isn't it. Now, what would provide the most dramatic demonstration? Removal of superfluous hair?
KATIE	I do not have superfluous hair. Besides, it hurts.
TIM	What then?
KATIE	Maybe you could do me a face job.
BOO-BOO	I don't think I have anything suitable with me.
KATIE	Nonsense, you don't need anything special. Simple country beauty preparations are best. I know - an egg-white face mask.
BOO-BOO	Is that good?
TIM	Have you ever seen a hen with wrinkles?
KATIE	This way, Primrose. We can fix it up in the

kitchen.

BOO-BOO   I hope I can do it. Is it something like an omelette?

                 (KATIE and BOO-BOO exit to kitchen. TIM
                 crosses, opens french windows and calls to
                 TASKLEY.)

TIM   Mr Taskley, are you there? P.P. ?

                 (TASKLEY opens top half of caravan door.)

TASKLEY   How the hell did I get in here? I just woke up
                 and....... (Sees tiger-skin.) Wow! I remember.

                 (Slams door shut again.)

TIM   Don't worry, P.P., I'll come and help you.

TASKLEY   (Opening window a crack.) Don't come out, Tim.
                 There's a tiger.

TIM   That's all right. I can deal with him.

TASKLEY   You sure?

TIM   I think you'd better duck out of sight. I don't
                 want you distracting him.

TASKLEY   I won't distract him. (Disappears from window.)

                 (TIM starts record of animals roaring, goes into
                 garden and rolls up the tiger-skin which he hides
                 in the bushes, all the time yelling at the supposed
                 tiger. He then rushes back into the house, fades
                 out record, takes blunderbuss from wall and
                 goes out to knock at caravan door.)

TIM   You can come out now.

TASKLEY   (off) Is it safe?

TIM   Coast's clear at the moment and anyway I have

a gun. By the way, Primrose Lane's arrived.
The mystery tour came back early.

TASKLEY   (Opening caravan door slightly.) I can't see very
                     well without my glasses. You're sure there's
                     nothing there?

TIM   Safe as my own back garden. What am I saying?
                     It is my own back garden.

TASKLEY   Keep me covered and I'll make a run for it.

                     (TASKLEY rushes into house, followed by TIM, who
                     lays down gun and closes french windows. TASK-
                     LEY flops into a chair.)

TIM   Are you all right, Mr Taskley? I know - a brandy.
                     (Pours brandy.) Mr Taskley, I know you've every
                     right to be annoyed at what happened but please
                     don't go to the police.

TASKLEY   The police? I intend to write to the Queen.

TIM   The Queen! Please don't Mr Taskley. I acted
                     without thinking.

TASKLEY   Without thinking? Don't be over-modest. What
                     you did was extremely courageous - dragging me
                     to safety and scaring off those beasts. I shall
                     insist on an award for gallantry from the Queen.

TIM   Oh that. Really it was nothing.

TASKLEY   True grit. Anyway, I think I'd better delay my
                     departure. Wouldn't like to run into one a second
                     time.

TIM   I think I can promise you you'll never see that
                     leopard again.

                     (MYRTLE, still in leopard outfit, enters front
                     door unseen by TASKLEY who has his back to her.
                     TIM rushes at her and forcibly removes her hat

and coat which he rolls up and holds behind his back.)

Let me take your coat.

MYRTLE   It's been lovely. I've been all round the country-side.

TIM   Quite a mystery tour, eh?

MYRTLE   Yes, indeed - a mystery tour.

TIM   Mr Taskley, this is -er.....

TASKLEY   How do you do, Miss Lane.

TIM   No, Mr Taskley, Primrose Lane is in the kitchen arranging a demonstration. This is -er......

TASKLEY   Could I have my spectacles back, then I'll see who I'm talking to.

TIM   Of course, P.P.   Here they are.

                (TIM gives TASKLEY his spectacles, which are lying on the desk, and crosses his fingers.)

TASKLEY   No introductions are necessary. I can sense that this is the lady I have come so far to meet.

MYRTLE   The stars were right. It is kismet.

TIM   Well, you two seem to be getting along splendidly. If you'll excuse me, I want to have a word with Sodworthy. I'll pop your coat into the caravan.

                (TIM takes gun, exits french windows and after putting coat and hat into caravan, disappears down garden.
                There is an embarrassed silence as MYRTLE and TASKLEY eye each other.)

MYRTLE   Please sit down, Mr Taskley. How is the bump on your head?

TASKLEY	(Feels head.) Well, it's a bit.... Say, that's fantastic! You're clairvoyant.
MYRTLE	A little. But how did you......?
TASKLEY	You really are the most wonderful person I've ever met.
MYRTLE	(Overcome.) Oh, Mr Taskley!
TASKLEY	A woman like you could be such an inspiration to me. You could influence my whole life.
MYRTLE	If only you'd let me try.
TASKLEY	I've always found it difficult to make decisions, but somehow I feel with your help the future might be easier.
MYRTLE	I'm sure it would.
TASKLEY	I know I'm presuming on our slight acquaintance, but would you......? No, it's too much to ask.
MYRTLE	Of course it isn't. Do go on.
TASKLEY	What I want to ask of you would mean such a disruption to your whole way of life. A change of residence..... (He is fiddling with his pen, which he drops. In picking it up he finds himself kneeling at MYRTLE's feet.) What I want to ask is....
MYRTLE	(breathlessly) Yes?
TASKLEY	(Rising.) No, I'm not being fair. I'm rushing you. I want you to know what you're letting yourself in for - how much work you'll have, the financial arrangements and so forth. I don't want you to say yes to something you'll regret.
MYRTLE	I know I shan't.

TASKLEY   Tell you what, I'll put all the details on paper and I want you to take your time and consider carefully before giving me your answer.

MYRTLE   There's no need, but if that's what you want.

TASKLEY   (Looking round.) Where's my briefcase? It must be in the caravan. I'll go and get it. (He pauses at the french windows.) I sure hope the answer's yes. (He exits french windows and makes for caravan. He is almost there when he remembers that there may be wild animals around.) Wow! The beasts! (Rushes into caravan and slams door.)

MYRTLE   Poor man, he's quite distracted. Perhaps I don't know my own sex-appeal. I must let Edith know. Oh golly gosh, I said I'd phone earlier. Telephone. Now where? Oh yes, I remember - in the cupboard. (She crosses to telephone cupboard and dials a number. She comes out of cupboard to make sure she is not being overheard and stays outside for conversation.) Edith, it's Myrtle... ...... Yes, everything's going fine, but I'm so excited - Cupid's dart has struck......... What do you mean, business first and day-dreams after? ...... Oh, all right...... Yes, I'm in Russell Spring's house. It was easier than I thought - they take in paying guests....... What?........ Have I met any of the 'Village Almanac' writers? Not yet, Edith...... Of course I know it's important. It seems so underhand though - living in the Spring house and trying to steal their writers to work for 'Aunt Ada's Journal' ...... Primrose Lane is in the kitchen so I'll get to work on her first, then tomorrow I'll try to meet the rest and sign them up........ Yes, Edith....... Now may I tell you my news. I've had a proposal of marriage...... No, I'm not drunk...... Just a minute, someone's coming. I'll close the door.

(As MYRTLE closes the door of telephone cupboard KATIE and BOO-BOO enter from kitchen with a bowl of whipped egg-whites.)

KATIE   It's a wonderful astringent. Natural products are
         best for the skin, don't you think? Look what
         asses' milk did for Cleopatra.

BOO-BOO I once had a bath in strawberry yoghourt - but I
         don't think I'd better tell you about that.

KATIE   (Placing chair near kitchen door and façing
         french windows.)   Is the light good enough here?
         I hope you don't mind an audience. We have a
         friend visiting.

         (TIM enters through french windows.)

         Primrose is all ready.   I'm sure she'd like to
         meet Mr Taskley.

TIM   Oh yes, Primrose, you must meet Mr Taskley.
         (Inadvertently points gun at BOO-BOO.)

BOO-BOO All right, I'll meet him, but there's no need to
         threaten me.

TIM   (Realising.) So sorry. I've just been seeing to a
         rat at the bottom of the garden. (to KATIE with
         relish) He's burrowing in that heap of manure at
         the moment.

KATIE   Poor little rat. I doubt if he'll like that.

TIM   Perfect camouflage for him I should think.

KATIE   Where is Mr Taskley?

TIM   I don't know why, but I saw him go in the caravan
         again. I'll fetch him.

         (TIM exits french windows and makes for the
         caravan, taking gun with him.)

KATIE   This might be rather messy. I'd better get a
         towel. Carry on beating that.

         (KATIE exits to kitchen. TIM knocks on caravan

door as BOO-BOO stares worriedly at bowl of
egg-white.)

TASKLEY   (Appearing at caravan window.) Thank God you're
               here. Came to look for my briefcase and forgot
               all about those damn carnivores. I was scared to
               come back,in case I got torn limb from limb.

TIM   It's all right, P.P., I've got my shooter. Prim-
               rose Lane's just going to give Katie a face pack,if
               you'd like to meet her.

TASKLEY   That's great. (Opens caravan door slightly.)
               You're sure it's all right to come out?

TIM   I'll cover you.

               (TASKLEY emerges from caravan and they cross
               to cottage.)

TASKLEY   Don't know how you manage to live here. I'd be
               scared stiff. How does old Sodworthy manage the
               garden?

TIM   He's quite safe. The animals don't like the way he
               smells.

               (TIM and TASKLEY enter french windows.)

               Mr Taskley, meet Primrose Lane.

BOO-BOO   How do you do?

               (KATIE enters from kitchen with towel.)

TASKLEY   Wow! You sure are an advertisement for the sim-
               ple country life. Early to bed and early to rise,
               eh?

BOO-BOO   Not very often.

TIM   Nonsense, P.P. She's up at 6am every morning
               to feed her goats. Makes a beautiful sight on the

side of the village common.

KATIE

But you always did like anything on the common side. Well, is everything ready, Primrose?

BOO-BOO

I think so.

KATIE

How do you want me to sit?

BOO-BOO

(Demonstrating.) If you sat down like this with your head back and put the towel round you like this.

(All are paying attention to BOO-BOO as ROGER comes up garden and enters french windows.)

ROGER

(In his own voice.) I've had just about enough of this.

(KATIE and TASKLEY turn to face ROGER. TIM, realising BOO-BOO must not be recognised by ROGER, plasters her face with the egg-white. She yells and KATIE turns.)

KATIE

(to TIM) Whatever did you do that for? That was for me. (to ROGER) Sodworthy, you really must learn to knock. What did you say?

ROGER

I said, 'I've had just about enough of it.'

KATIE

(to TIM) He had just about enough, Tim. Could you order some more manure?

TIM

Certainly, Katie. Sweets to the sweet.

KATIE

Carry on with what's there, Sodworthy, and no more interruptions or the master might turn nasty.

ROGER

(Touching forelock and again in rustic voice.)
Yes, ma'am. Sorry, ma'am.

TIM

Remember the old country saying, Adam - 'If you wish your life to keep, spread your dung till ankle-deep. '

ROGER   Aaaar! (ROGER exits down garden.)

BOO-BOO   (In a small voice.) Can I take this off now?

KATIE   Yes, of course, Primrose. Thank you very much
                 for showing me.

                 (BOO-BOO rises and removes towel.)

TASKLEY   (Eyeing BOO-BOO's figure.) Even with your face
                 covered, Miss Lane, you're still a humdinger.

BOO-BOO   Thank you.

KATIE   Let me guide you upstairs to get cleaned up.

                 (Leads BOO-BOO to stairs.)

BOO-BOO   You'd better. I think I'm turning into a meringue.

                 (KATIE picks up BOO-BOO's small case and both
                 exit upstairs.)

TIM   (Picking up bowl and towel.) I'll just clear this out
                 of the way.

TASKLEY   Oh Tim, I never did find my briefcase. I have a
                 letter I must write.

TIM   Right there where you left it when you brought in
                 the magazines.

TASKLEY   Gee, so it is. I forgot. (Picks up briefcase.) Do
                 you have an envelope?

TIM   Yes, of course. Have a seat at the desk. There's
                 everything you want there.

TASKLEY   Thank you.

                 (TIM exits to kitchen. TASKLEY takes paper

from briefcase, sits at desk and starts to write.
MYRTLE emerges from telephone cupboard and
gives a small ecstatic gasp as she sees TASKLEY.)

I'm sorry. I didn't see you.

MYRTLE   Please don't let me disturb you. I'm going to my
                          room, I mean my caravan, to lie down. My heart
                          is going pit-a-pat.

TASKLEY   Is it serious?

MYRTLE   (Romantically.) Very serious.

TASKLEY   You're not going to lie down by yourself?

MYRTLE   (Flirtatiously.) Oh, Mr Taskley, that really is
                          naughty of you. There is always a certain amount
                          of tension at such times, but we must keep our
                          feelings in check.

TASKLEY   I'm about to put my proposal to you on paper,

                          (Another gasp from MYRTLE.)

                          but before I do I insist on escorting you. Now
                          I've found you I intend to take great care nothing
                          happens to you.

                          (TASKLEY picks up the gun and he and MYRTLE
                          exit french windows and make for caravan.)

MYRTLE   What a sense of humour you have, but how very
                          romantic to have you riding shotgun. (Pausing in
                          caravan doorway.) À bientôt.

TASKLEY   Bye.

                          (MYRTLE closes caravan door and TASKLEY
                          creeps warily back into cottage, closing windows
                          behind him. He sits down at desk and starts to
                          write. ROGER comes up garden and peers in
                          french windows. When he is seen by TASKLEY,

ROGER indicates that he wishes to see KATIE.
TASKLEY motions for him to wait and calls upstairs for KATIE.)

Katie? You there? I think old Adam would like
a word with you.

(TASKLEY returns to his writing and KATIE
comes downstairs.)

KATIE   Thank you. I'll go and see what he wants.

TASKLEY   Outside? But the beasts......?

KATIE   I'm all right with Adam there.

TASKLEY   I forgot. They don't like the way he smells.

KATIE   I don't like it much myself.

(KATIE exits french windows to ROGER while
TASKLEY continues writing.)

Poor Roger. Is it dreadful out here?

ROGER   Do you know what he's got me doing? Shovelling
bloody ....

KATIE   (Interrupting.) It's probably doing you good.
Healthy exercise puts roses in your cheeks.

ROGER   Unfortunately it's not roses I'm shovelling.

KATIE   If it makes you feel any better just think you're
doing it for me. And if the rhubarb could speak
I'm sure it would say thank you too.

ROGER   I'll never touch rhubarb again. Katie, I'm so
miserable.

KATIE   Poor Roger.

ROGER   Being out here has given me time to think and I

> know I'm missing Boo-Boo. Perhaps she won't
> come back to me and even if she does she won't
> stay - I'll probably smell like this for weeks.
> There should be an Unmarriage Guidance Council
> for people like me.

KATIE   Perhaps there is.

ROGER   I might even write to Evelyn Home about it.

KATIE   Roger, I've just thought. Perhaps if you had a
               word about your problems with the woman who
               answers readers' letters in Tim's magazine.

ROGER   Do you think it would do any good?

KATIE   Of course it would. I'll phone Mrs -Er, I mean
               Madge Playfair right away and get her to come
               round.

ROGER   I don't think I can wait.

KATIE   But you must. And I think you should carry on
               with the muck-spreading. It's making you think
               and that's good.

ROGER   I can't meet her dressed like this.

KATIE   That's the whole point. She's a very simple
               countrywoman. You'll get the best out of her just
               as you are. Now, off you go and stop worrying.

ROGER   (Heaving a great sigh.) All right then.

               (KATIE watches ROGER go down the garden then
               re-enters cottage.)

KATIE   Sorry to disturb you, Mr Taskley. Old Adam has
               a bit of a problem and I'm going to phone Madge
               Playfair, Tim's advice columnist, so that he can
               talk it over with her.

TASKLEY   Go right ahead. I'd love to meet her.

(TIM enters from kitchen.)

KATIE   Darling, I'm just going to give Madge Playfair a
               ring and have her round.

TIM   (Mystified.) Well, if you think she'll come.

KATIE   I'm sure she will. Won't be a moment.

               (KATIE enters telephone cupboard and closes door.)

TASKLEY   (Sealing letter.) I wonder if you'd give this to
               Deirdre for me? (Lays letter on desk beside
               envelope containing last page of serial.)

TIM   Of course. (Picks up wrong envelope and puts it
               in his pocket.) You like her?

TASKLEY   I like her a lot. I wonder which planet she was
               born under. Don't suppose it was Venus?

TIM   I think Pluto's more likely.

TASKLEY   Now Primrose Lane is something completely
               different. Do you suppose she would agree to be
               our 'Dish of the Month' in 'Fleshpot'?

TIM   You mean pose in the nude? I doubt it.

TASKLEY   Don't be too sure. A lot of shy young ladies
               change their minds pretty quickly when they see
               how well we pay. To save embarrassment and
               getting my face slapped too often I've these forms
               printed. Short and to the point. (Produces form
               and reads:) '£1000 for your nude photo in my
               magazine. Sign here if interested.' (Puts form
               in envelope and lays it beside his previous letter.)
               Perhaps you'd pass it on for me.

TIM   Certainly, though I doubt if it'll do any good.

TASKLEY   Gosh, my head hurts. I think I hit it on the floor
               when that leopard attacked me.

(KATIE emerges from telephone cupboard.)

KATIE   That's it settled then. Madge Playfair will be
                    dropping in shortly.

TASKLEY   That's swell. I'm delighted.

TIM   I'm looking forward to seeing her myself. Katie,
                    can we do anything about Mr Taskley's head? It's
                    still sore where he bumped it.

KATIE   Yes, I'm sure we . . . .

TASKLEY   (Interrupting.) Say, perhaps Sister Truscott
                    could give me something for it.

TIM   )
KATIE)   (together) Sister Truscott?

TASKLEY   Do you think she's finished her evening rounds on
                    her bicycle?

KATIE   We don't really see very much of her. She just
                    pops in with her monthly column.

TASKLEY   I must say I've enjoyed meeting old Adam, Prim-
                    rose and Deirdre, and I'm sure Madge Playfair is
                    a treat in store, but I feel I can't really make up
                    my mind about syndication unless I meet Sister
                    Truscott. I mean, how do I know you don't write
                    her column yourself?

TIM   Ridiculous. (Laughs loudly.)

TASKLEY   Of course. (Joins in the laughter which hurts
                    his head.) Ouch! My head's splitting.

KATIE   Tell you what - why don't you go upstairs to the
                    guestroom and lie down while we try to contact
                    Sister Truscott? It's the first door you come to
                    at the top of the stairs. Make yourself at home.

TASKLEY   Yes, I think I might do that. (Starting to mount stairs.) You'll give me a call if I'm not down when Madge arrives. (sudden thought) Say - the big cats!

TIM   No problem. Mrs Playfair has a degree in animal psychology.

TASKLEY   What do you know! (Exits upstairs.)

TIM   What the hell are you doing? He hadn't asked to meet Madge Playfair. Why complicate things?

KATIE   It was the only way I could get Roger to stay.

TIM   Now Roger wants to meet Madge Playfair? Is he having a problem page on his yoghourt cartons? This isn't a game, Katie. We're in a jam, fighting for our bread and butter.

KATIE   Is that next month's pudding recipe?

TIM   I'll ignore that. The point is that you have suggested to Taskley that he meets Madge Playfair. (Emphasising each word.) We do not have a Madge Playfair.

KATIE   Mrs -Er.

TIM   Mrs -Er? Don't be ridiculous. Besides, she wouldn't come.

KATIE   I've told her we've got her money.

TIM   But we haven't.

KATIE   I'll think of something.

TIM   You'd better. My nerves are like chewed string. I could do with a month in hospital. Hospital! What about Sister Truscott?

KATIE   Maybe we could manage without her now we've got Madge.

TIM   We can't. You heard what the man said - no Sister
                Truscott, no contracts. It's just too much. I give
                up.

KATIE   You can't give up now.

TIM   The plain fact is that lucky as we've been with our
                charade so far, we cannot run to a cast of thou-
                sands.

KATIE   You don't suppose Primrose......?

TIM   Do me a favour. After the face-pack episode I
                should think she'll walk straight out, besides
                which,Taskley would recognise her.

KATIE   So after all this mad panic we're no further for-
                ward?

TIM   (Patting pocket.) Well,I do have a contract for
                Myrtle's horoscopes and (indicating envelope on
                desk) an invitation to pose in the nude for 'Flesh-
                pot'.

KATIE   (Picking up envelope from desk.) Do you think
                America is ready for your naked body?

TIM   Not mine. Boo- .... I mean Primrose's.
                (Takes envelope and pockets it.)

KATIE   I refuse to surrender till we're found out. What
                does a district nurse wear?

TIM   A bedpan and bicycle clips?

KATIE   There's my wig upstairs and I'm sure we could...

TIM   Let's deal with the wardrobe later. It's the cast-
                ing that worries me.

KATIE   The casting couch you mean.

TIM   Come again?

KATIE   If I find you and Primrose snuggling up together I
                 can throw her out of the house.

TIM   That won't help.

KATIE   She's got nowhere else to go. Kit her out as the
                 new district nurse who I'm not supposed to have
                 met, and Bob's your Sister.

TIM   It might work.

KATIE   It's got to.

                 (BOO-BOO enters and starts to come downstairs.)

                 Whoops, end of conversation. Why hello, Prim-
                 rose. Egg-white certainly works wonders.

TIM   You look radiant.

KATIE   Doesn't she just! I must try one myself.

BOO-BOO   It was horrible. I don't think one of the eggs was
                 quite fresh.

KATIE   I am glad you came, Primrose. Your work sounds
                 fascinating and I'd love to hear more about it.
                 Come and sit down.

BOO-BOO   No more practical jokes?

TIM   Do we look as if we would.

                 (BOO-BOO sits warily.)

KATIE   Tim, did you send the last page of the serial to
                 Pritchard?

TIM   Hell no. I'd better nip out and post it now. I
                 haven't addressed it.

KATIE   I'll do it. I feel like a breath of fresh air. (Stamps
                 and addresses letter remaining on desk.)

TIM   Thanks very much.

KATIE   Why don't you get Primrose a drink, (meaning-
                        fully) then you can both have a cosy little chat while
                        I'm out.

TIM   Good idea. What'll you have to drink, Primrose?

BOO-BOO   I don't think I want anything.

KATIE   Nonsense. It doesn't go on your bill. This is on
                        the house. (Picks up letter.) Won't be a tick, the
                        box is at the end of the road.

                        (KATIE makes elaborate signs to TIM and exits
                        front door.)

TIM   What'll it be then?

BOO-BOO   Nothing thanks. Really. I never drink when I'm
                        depressed.

TIM   But you mustn't be depressed. (Sits beside her.)
                        My little Boo-Boo mustn't be depressed.

                        (TIM puts his arm round BOO-BOO but she rises.)

BOO-BOO   (Working up to tears.) I'm missing Roger. I
                        know he gets angry with me sometimes, but I
                        haven't seen him for one whole day and I'm so
                        miserable.

TIM   (Crossing to her.) What you need is a shoulder to
                        cry on.

                        (Proffers his, but BOO-BOO takes no notice. TIM
                        realises that more complex measures are called
                        for. BOO-BOO continues to cry, making the most
                        awful faces.)

                        You know, you're beautiful when you cry.

BOO-BOO   (Recovering.) I am?

TIM   Have you ever done any acting?

BOO-BOO   I once did a commercial for Playtex but they didn't show my face.

TIM   But you have a classical face. Lady Macbeth. Yes, that's it - Lady Macbeth. I've got a friend who's setting up a film just now. I'm sure he'd be interested.

BOO-BOO   You think so?

TIM   I'm sure. And I know you can do it. Go up to the top of the stairs.

BOO-BOO   (Warily.) What for? It's some sort of trick.

TIM   All right. If you don't want a career in films....

             (BOO-BOO runs to top of stairs.)

BOO-BOO   I'm sorry. What is it you want me to do?

TIM   This is the sleep-walking scene. I want you to hold your head up, hold your arms out like this, close your eyes and walk regally down the stairs. (TIM demonstrates.)

BOO-BOO   You really think your friend would be interested?

TIM   Of course. Now close your eyes and walk down.

             (BOO-BOO follows instructions and walks un-certainly down stairs.)

             Hold your head up. Remember you're a queen. Your arms a little further apart.

             (TIM positions himself so that BOO-BOO's out-stretched arms pass on each side of him. At the moment of collision Katie quickly-enters front door.)

KATIE   So this is what you get up to the minute my
                            back's turned.

BOO-BOO   But I was only ... We were only ... Tell
                            her, Tim.

KATIE   You certainly haven't wasted much time.
                            Get your things immediately, and if you're
                            not out of this house in five minutes you'll
                            find yourself principal witness in a divorce
                            case. As it is, I'll make sure that you're
                            struck off the Hathaway register. (to TIM)
                            I'll have something to say to you later.
                            (Exits kitchen door.)

BOO-BOO   Why didn't you tell her we were only
                            rehearsing?

TIM   You saw the mood she was in. She wouldn't
                            listen.

BOO-BOO   What am I going to do? You said the last
                            bus had gone. Where am I going to sleep?

TIM   Don't worry. I really feel partly to blame
                            for what has happened so I'll help you. Now
                            listen carefully. We were expecting the new
                            district nurse to stay the night. Katie hasn't
                            met her, so if you pretend to be Sister
                            Truscott you could sleep here and leave on
                            the first bus in the morning.

BOO-BOO   But Katie would know it was me.

TIM   I think your brains are in your bust. You'd
                            have to be disguised.

BOO-BOO   I see. But what could I wear?

                            (BOO-BOO turns away and a rolled up blue
                            overall is thrown through the kitchen door
                            to TIM.)

TIM   Well, there's this for a start.

BOO-BOO   That was quick.

TIM   And there's plenty of other things upstairs.

Come and I'll show you. I wish we had a thermometer.

(TIM leads BOO-BOO to the stairs.)

BOO-BOO

I don't think I can do it. I don't know anything about nursing.

TIM

I'll help out. Just do what I say.

BOO-BOO

(Alarmed.) I've just thought. When I was a beauty demonstrator your wife wanted a facial. Now I'm a nurse you don't think she'll ask for an anemone?

TIM

I doubt it. Come on.

(TIM and BOO-BOO exit upstairs. KATIE enters from kitchen with a cup of coffee. She crosses and goes through french windows to garden.)

KATIE

(Calling.) Mr Sodworthy! Adam! (In a lower tone.) Roger!

(ROGER appears from the bottom of the garden.)

How's the muck spreading going?

ROGER

Is that a cup of coffee? Right now I'd give you a hundred pounds for it.

KATIE

That's not necessary. You can have it for ten.

ROGER

It's a deal. (Takes coffee.)

KATIE

Good. (Holds out hand for money.)

ROGER

You don't mean it?

KATIE

I'm afraid I do. Please, Roger. I'll explain later.

ROGER

(Giving KATIE the money.) I don't know why I'm doing this. It's all a horrible nightmare.

KATIE

Thank you, Roger. You'll never regret this.

ROGER   I regret it already.

KATIE   I'd have made you a sandwich but the bread's
                 finished.

                 (MYRTLE enters.)

MYRTLE   Did I hear someone mention sandwiches?

KATIE   I hope not.

MYRTLE   Doesn't matter now. I'm too excited to eat.

ROGER   (Handing cup back to KATIE.) Thank 'ee kindly,
                 ma'am. Most heartwarmin'.

MYRTLE   You must be Adam Sodworthy. I'd love to have a
                 chat with you. Do you enjoy working here?

ROGER   Don't get me started on that.

KATIE   No, don't get him started on that. He's so enthus-
                 iastic he'll keep you talking for hours.

                 (TIM comes downstairs and sees group outside.)

TIM   Is that Sodworthy outside? Tell him if he's fin-
                 ished with the manure, the septic tank wants
                 spring cleaning.

                 (ROGER takes off down garden.)

KATIE   (Shouting after him.) I'll give you a call when
                 Mrs Playfair arrives.

MYRTLE   What a willing worker. Is that your husband? I
                 must see if he knows anything about a billetdoux
                 I am expecting.

                 (As MYRTLE and KATIE enter the cottage,
                 TASKLEY comes downstairs.)

                 Why, Mr Taskley!

TIM   Are you feeling any better?

TASKLEY   Just a little, perhaps.

KATIE   Sister Truscott will be here shortly. I'm sure
                            she'll be able to help.

MYRTLE   Sister Truscott? I'd very much like to meet her.
                            And did I hear you say that Madge Playfair was
                            coming?

TASKLEY   You must all be such old friends.

TIM   We see them, of course, but sometimes months
                            pass and they never bump into each other.

MYRTLE   (Flirtatiously.) Your missive has not reached me,
                            Mr Taskley. I hope you haven't reconsidered.

TASKLEY   Of course not. I gave it to.......

TIM   Yes, well I -er .... Here you are.

                            (TIM reluctantly gives MYRTLE envelope from
                            his pocket.)

MYRTLE   Thank you. I shall read it in my Romany bower.
                            (Makes for windows.)

TASKLEY   (Picking up gun.) Let me escort you.

MYRTLE   (With a laugh.) In case I am molested? How
                            gallant!

                            (TASKLEY looks warily round garden, then rushes
                            MYRTLE into caravan and closes door.)

TIM   Damn! She's got his contract. We'll have to get
                            it back.

KATIE   How's Sister Truscott?

TIM   Everything's under control. I gave her full per-

mission to pillage your wardrobe. You'd better go
in the kitchen so she can make an entrance.

KATIE   (Making for kitchen.) I'm almost starting to enjoy
               this! (Exits through kitchen door.)

TIM   (At foot of stairs.)   Psssst!

BOO-BOO   (off) Can I come down now?

TIM   Coast's clear.

               (BOO-BOO comes downstairs. She is wearing the
               blue overall, spectacles, a dark wig, a bride's
               head-dress with short veil, pair of wellington
               boots and carries a black bag.)

BOO-BOO   How do I look?

TIM   Like the agricultural wedding of the year - but
               there isn't time to do anything about it now. I
               want you to go outside, count up to five hundred,
               then ring the doorbell.

BOO-BOO   I don't think it's going to work. She's bound to
               recognise either me or the clothes.

TIM   Nonsense. If you're not sure what to say or do,
               take your lead from me.

               (Bundles BOO-BOO out of front door.)

               I wish we had a thermometer. (Crosses to open
               kitchen door.) You can come out now.

KATIE   (Entering.) How's it going?

TIM   She's outside the front door complete with little
               black bag. I should warn you that she's wearing
               your wedding veil.

KATIE   Of all the nerve.

(Caravan door opens and TASKLEY emerges.)

TIM   Sssh! Here's Taskley now.

TASKLEY   I don't want you to make a hasty decision. Read
                 it carefully and think it over.

MYRTLE   (In doorway.) I will. (She closes caravan door.)

                 (TASKLEY looks cautiously round for wild beasts,
                 then rushes back into the cottage,with the gun,and
                 slams the french windows.)

TASKLEY   What a weirdo! I just love the way she talks.
                 Nutty as a fruit cake, but what does that matter
                 so long as she delivers the goods.

KATIE   It looks as though you're going to be able to see
                 Madge Playfair in action. Old Adam has a prob-
                 lem he wants to discuss with her when she comes
                 round. We thought you could perhaps hide in the
                 telephone cupboard and eavesdrop.

TASKLEY   That would be swell.

TIM   You've really made up your mind to stick to the
                 magazine side of the business, then?

TASKLEY   Almost certainly, so long as I like the rest of
                 your staff and my new astrologer says the signs
                 are right.

TIM   Good. (Doorbell rings.) My, my,that sounds
                 like somebody now. (He opens front door.) Why,
                 it's Sister Truscott!

BOO-BOO   509, 510, 511 ...... Oh!

TIM   Do come in, Sister Truscott.

                 (BOO-BOO enters.)

KATIE   Sister Truscott, how lovely to see you.

TIM	(to TASKLEY) You see the quaint old English costume our district nurses wear. We call them the 'Brides of Medicine'.
TASKLEY	Gee, that's cute.
TIM	Sister Truscott, this is Mr Taskley, who is over from the States on a business trip.
TASKLEY	Happy to meet you. Say, got any babies in that little black bag of yours?
BOO-BOO	(to TIM) Should I have?
	(TIM signals 'No'.)
	No.
KATIE	Mr Taskley has fallen and bumped his head. Maybe you can do something to help.
TASKLEY	I feel a little feverish. Perhaps you should take my temperature.
TIM	This being a social call I doubt if she'll have a thermometer with her.
BOO-BOO	Oh yes I have. (Produces a large wooden wall thermometer and whispers to TIM.) Wasn't it luck I found this on the wall outside.
TASKLEY	(Alarmed.) Just where do you intend to put that?
KATIE	(Interrupting.) Perhaps you should take Mr Taskley's pulse.
	(BOO-BOO does so.)
TASKLEY	I do appreciate your coming here through all these animals.
BOO-BOO	(Surprised.) Oh, you mean the cows?

TIM

Isn't it silly, she's more scared of cows than anything. Of course, her bicycle scares off the rest.

TASKLEY

You're certainly a game one. An article from you about the wild things you encounter on your rounds would knock out our readers. May I sign you up for a monthly column in my magazine 'Home Spun'?

(TIM nods vigorously.)

BOO-BOO

Yes, if you like.

TASKLEY

That's what I like. I admire quick decisions. (Getting briefcase.) I have an agreement here, if you'd care to put your name to it.

(TASKLEY gets out printed contract and a pen. BOO-BOO is gazing vacantly into space.)

Right here on the dotted line.

(No response from BOO-BOO.)

Is anything the matter?

BOO-BOO

I'm sorry. It's just that I'm not myself at the moment. Where do you want me to sign?

TIM

(With great stress as he points.) There. E. Truscott, S.R.N.

(BOO-BOO signs.)

TASKLEY

Thanks a million. I'm sorry you're not feeling at your best.

KATIE

Would you like a cup of tea?

BOO-BOO

That wouldn't do any good. If you want to know, I'm having rather an unhappy love affair and that's what's upsetting me.

TASKLEY	Have you had a word with Madge about it?
	(BOO-BOO looks at TIM who shakes his head.)
BOO-BOO	No.
TASKLEY	Don't you think it would be a good idea?
	(KATIE nods, TIM shakes his head. BOO-BOO sees only KATIE and replies:)
BOO-BOO	Yes.
TASKLEY	Nothing like a word with an understanding old friend when it comes to an affaire of the heart, eh?
BOO-BOO	I suppose so.
	(Door slams off.)
KATIE	That was the back door. She's here. I'll just give Adam a call.
TIM	Both at the same time? Do you think that's wise?
KATIE	Group therapy. It's all the rage. (Obviously.) Mr Taskley, didn't you say you have an important telephone call to make?
TASKLEY	I don't think so. Oh yes, I see what you mean. Yes, I have to call New York right away.
TIM	For God's sake reverse the charges.
KATIE	(Indicating cupboard.) The telephone is in there, P.P.
TASKLEY	Thank you, Katie.
	(TASKLEY enters telephone cupboard and shuts the door.)
KATIE	Don't be shy, Sister. Tell Madge all about your

problems. Tim and I will go upstairs and leave you in private.

TIM   Hadn't we better stay?

KATIE   I'm stage-managing this. Upstairs!

(TIM goes to top of stairs. KATIE crosses to french windows and calls down garden:)

Adam! Mrs Playfair's here.

(KATIE signals to TIM to leave - which he does. She then takes a cushion to the top of the stairs, throws it over on to the floor and exits. Immediately MRS -ER enters from kitchen, shakes up cushion and replaces it. She then sees BOO-BOO.)

MRS -ER   Is Mrs Spring -er?

BOO-BOO   She's just gone upstairs.

MRS -ER   Then I'll wait.

(MRS -ER takes a seat. There is a silence,during which MRS -ER examines BOO-BOO minutely.)

Is somebody not feeling very -er?

BOO-BOO   Everybody's fine. Except me.

MRS -ER   And what might be the matter with -er?

BOO-BOO   I'm so depressed. My boyfriend's broken it off.

MRS -ER   Shouldn't worry about that. Men are more bother than they're -er.

BOO-BOO   I'll probably never see him again.

(ROGER enters french windows.)

MRS -ER	What do you -er?
ROGER	Been doin' a bit o' work for Mrs Spring. She told me......
MRS -ER	(Interrupting.) Better sit down and -er. (Sniffs.) On second thoughts, better stand over -er. (Indicates other side of room.)
	(There is a long silence.)
BOO-BOO	Should I phone him?
MRS -ER	Phone who?
BOO-BOO	My boyfriend.
MRS -ER	That depends. Why did he -er?
BOO-BOO	He thinks I'm always flirting with other men.
MRS -ER	And are you?
BOO-BOO	Of course I'm not. They do all the flirting. It's all one-sided.
MRS -ER	I see.
BOO-BOO	Some of them say the most awful things, but I'm not good at making clever answers, so I just stand there like a lemon.
ROGER	More like a peach, I'd say.
BOO-BOO	You see he's doing it too.
ROGER	Must be a funny chap you go out with if he doesn't like other fellows paying you compliments.
BOO-BOO	He likes me to get all dressed up, then gets jealous if anybody looks at me.
MRS -ER	That's the human race for you. As two-faced as a -er. (Makes vagues gesture with her hands.)

ROGER   A double-sided mirror.

BOO-BOO   You mean they see your virtues as they really are
                 but magnify your faults.

ROGER   That's good, that is. Very deep. I think that
                 helps me to understand things better too.

BOO-BOO   You've had the same problem?

ROGER   In a way. I was going to ask about it, but I've
                 seen it all from the ladies' side now. I shouldn't
                 be a-goin' on at my woman for flaunting herself -
                 I should be glad she's mine and not nobody else's.

BOO-BOO   And I can see that my boyfriend's been worried
                 that my head's going to be turned by all the com-
                 pliments because I haven't shown him they don't
                 mean anything to me and it's only him that matters.

MRS -ER   It's as clear as the nose on your -er. (Slaps hip.)
                 You've been far too -er.

ROGER   Jealous. Yes I have.

BOO-BOO   And I haven't been understanding enough. But I
                 will be from now on.

ROGER   Thank 'ee kindly for them words o'wisdom, ma'am.
                 I be gettin' back 'ome some'ow to make things all
                 right with my woman. (Makes for french windows.)
                 A double-sided mirror - that's deep. (Exits french
                 windows and goes down garden.)

MRS -ER   It was you that said it.

BOO-BOO   I'm not wasting any time either. I'll leave my
                 uniform upstairs and get to London tonight even
                 if I have to hitch a lift. I must see Roger.
                 (Going up stairs.) I didn't know I'd been magni-
                 fying his faults. Thank you for your help. (Exits.)

MRS -ER   Don't know why everybody's thanking me.

(TASKLEY enters from telephone cupboard.)

And who might you be?

TASKLEY | My name is Taskley and I'm on business from the States. I couldn't help overhearing just now. 'Man's thoughts are like a double-sided mirror, reflecting only what he wants to see'. I've never heard it put better.

MRS -ER | I never said that.

TASKLEY | Don't be over-modest. You're a very understand-ing woman, but then, of course, if you weren't you wouldn't have your present job.

MRS -ER | That's for sure. I sometimes wonder if I'm -er.

TASKLEY | Wasted here? Well, perhaps you are. (Winces and puts hand on head.) Excuse me. I have such a dreadful headache.

MRS -ER | What you need is a -er.

TASKLEY | A private consultation.

MRS -ER | Pardon?

TASKLEY | It's kind of you to offer.

MRS -ER | I came because Mrs Spring said she had my -er.

TASKLEY | Interests at heart. Indeed yes. As I do myself.

(TIM and KATIE enter and come downstairs.)

TIM | Well, you two seem to have met so there's no need for any introductions.

KATIE | (to MRS -ER) Here's the ten pounds I promised you.

MRS -ER | It's a good -er.

TIM   Cause. Yes, a very good cause.

TASKLEY   How wonderful to think that helping others gives
                    you such pleasure.

MRS -ER   I find it's more of a necessity than a -er.

TASKLEY   A necessity to help others. How unselfish. And
                    what is the money you're collecting helping to
                    support?

TIM   Mentally-deficient widows with word-blindness.

TASKLEY   (Producing wallet.) May I be allowed to con-
                    tribute? I'm sure you'd find another ten pounds
                    a great help.

KATIE   Mr Taskley you don't have to give her anything.

TASKLEY   My pleasure. (Hands ten pounds to MRS -ER.)

MRS -ER   (Brightening visibly.) That's really most -er.
                    Well, now I'm here I might as well make myself
                    -er. Can I get you a cup of tea and an aspirin
                    for your -er?

TASKLEY   That's very gracious of you. Perhaps I could
                    come and talk with you while you make it. Your
                    whole attitude to life refreshes me.

TIM   You've met all our friends and colleagues now,
                    P.P. I'm sure the rest is mere formality.

TASKLEY   I hope so, Tim. I'm reasonably happy about it
                    all, but I would welcome a little more guidance -
                    some sign from the astral plane.

MRS -ER   If you'd like to come through I'll see about that
                    -er, if that's all right by you, Mrs Spring.

KATIE   Please use the kitchen as if it were your own.
                    I think you know where everything is.

MRS -ER   I should do by this -er.

                        (TASKLEY and MRS -ER exit to kitchen.)

TIM   I've really got to hand it to you. Never thought
                        that old rat-bag would convince Taskley. I was
                        ready to come rushing downstairs and confess all.

KATIE   Don't get carried away, we're not out of the wood
                        yet. We need contracts..... signatures. And
                        now Roger and Primrose are threatening to leave
                        to hitch lifts to London. This whole thing could
                        still blow up in our faces.

TIM   I don't think I can stand the strain. It's like
                        trying to get a brazil nut out of the shell in one
                        piece.

KATIE   Well,grab the nutcrackers - here comes Roger
                        now and, oh no, he's cleaned up.

                        (ROGER enters french windows, he has washed
                        and tidied and looks reasonably presentable though
                        almost speechless with rage.)

TIM   Roger! Hello, old man. What brings you here?
                        Nice to see you. Have a drink.

KATIE   Tim, I must tell you - Roger's been here all
                        afternoon.

TIM   He has?

ROGER   You know damn well I have.

KATIE   Tim, you know that load of manure Roger sent
                        me for my birthday. Well,he arrived here and
                        insisted on spreading it without your knowing and
                        you took him for the new gardener.

TIM   And he kept it up all this time and I never sus-
                        pected? Roger, you are the world's greatest
                        practical joker.

KATIE
And he's spread all the manure. Roger, what can I say?

ROGER
I don't know about you, but I'm going to say plenty. There's a law about threatening people with shotguns, you know. However, I don't think I need the police. I'll settle this myself.

(ROGER walks menacingly towards TIM.)

When I've finished with your face it'll make steak tartare look well done.

TIM
You know I can't stand physical violence.

KATIE
Roger, please. You're much stronger than Tim. You'll kill him.

ROGER
You can bury him in the garden then. He'll have the best fertilised grave in the country.

(ROGER grabs TIM and is about to take a swing at him when BOO-BOO, in her own clothes, enters and runs downstairs.)

BOO-BOO
Roger, it's you.

(ROGER leaves go of TIM and BOO-BOO rushes into his arms.)

Oh Roger, I've missed you. (Sniffs.) Pooh, you smell a bit offensive.

ROGER
I feel a bit offensive.

KATIE
You two know each other?

BOO-BOO
I came here to find you and they've been horrid to me and covered me in eggs and made me be district nurses and Lady Macbeth and please take me home.

ROGER
I certainly will, Boo-Boo, just as soon as I've....

KATIE   Boo-Boo! (to TIM) You might have let me know.

TIM   It seemed simpler not to.

ROGER   I don't know what the hell you two have been play-
                    ing at but it'll cost you a bomb in damages. I'll
                    see my solicitor tomorrow.

TIM   Talk about ingratitude. After all we've done for
                    you.

ROGER   All you've done for us? Tell me just one thing.

KATIE   We've brought you together again.

TIM   We had to play these little scenes to stop you
                    rushing off.

KATIE   That's right. We wanted you to meet Mrs -Er, I
                    mean Madge Playfair because we thought she could
                    make you both see sense.

TIM   I'm sure you understand each other much better
                    now.

BOO-BOO   It's true, Roger. I haven't shown you I love you
                    enough and that made you jealous of anyone who
                    spoke to me.

ROGER   (Calming down.) And I was too distrustful and
                    started all the arguments.

BOO-BOO   Forgive me, Roger.

ROGER   Forgive me, Boo-Boo.

                    (ROGER and BOO-BOO embrace.)

KATIE   (to TIM) Quick thinking. Now what do we do?

ROGER   I'm sorry for what I said - what you did was for
                    true friendship. If there's ever anything we can
                    do for you in return.......

TIM   Well, there is one small item.

ROGER   You mean right now?

KATIE   Please, Roger.

BOO-BOO   We'll do it.

ROGER   All right. Tell me the worst.

TIM   Mr Taskley, whom you've both met, is here to do
                a business deal with me. It seems he's mistaken
                you for Adam Sodworthy and Primrose Lane, two
                of Village Almanac's contributors.

KATIE   We can't think how it happened.

TIM   It would be rather embarrassing to have to explain
                the mistake to him, so we'd like you to stay as you
                were for just a little longer.

BOO-BOO   When he thought I was Sister Truscott he got me to
                sign a contract for a magazine.

TIM   And if he asks you, that's exactly what we'd like
                you to do again - only this time sign Primrose
                Lane. O.K?

BOO-BOO   How many m's in Primrose?

TIM   Just one. Why don't you have a practice.

                (TIM takes paper from envelope in his pocket and
                passes it to BOO-BOO with a pen.)

                Sign along the bottom there. Primrose Lane.

                (BOO-BOO signs.)

                Perfect. (He puts paper back in his pocket. to
                ROGER) And you will have to sign Adam Sodworthy.
                Will you do it?

ROGER   Only if you'll lend me your car to get back to

London tonight.

TIM   (Throwing ROGER car keys.) It's a deal.

KATIE   You don't have to dirty yourself up again, but I
                         did like the accent. Could you do it again?

ROGER   Aaarrr! (Tugging forelock.)

TIM   All set? Action! (TIM calls through hatch.)
                         Mr Taskley, Adam and Primrose would like to be
                         getting off home now.

TASKLEY   (off) Be right with you.

TIM   Now, he is a little peculiar, so if he mentions any-
                         thing about leopards and tigers just ignore it.

ROGER   Why should he say anything about leopards and
                         tigers?

KATIE   Sssh!

                         (TASKLEY enters from kitchen.)

TASKLEY   That tea's helped my headache but (feeling head)
                         I've got one hell of a lump. Madge tells me some
                         butter rubbed on it will help. Now, to business.
                         I imagine Tim has explained the whole proposition
                         to you.

BOO-BOO   Well.......

TIM   In detail.

TASKLEY   So, if you're agreeable, I'd like you to sign these
                         contracts.

                         (Gets forms from briefcase and passes one each
                         to ROGER and BOO-BOO, after filling in details.)

                         Hardly knew you, Adam.

ROGER   I bain't very special when I'm workin' but aarrh,
                 I do clean up nice.

TASKLEY   If you'd just sign there.

ROGER   Thank 'ee sir, tis a great honour. (He signs.)

TASKLEY   Miss Lane?

BOO-BOO   Oh yes. Thank you very much. (She signs.)

TASKLEY   (Collecting forms.) That's most satisfactory. I
                 hope the beginning of a long association. Well,
                 I guess I'd better be getting back next door to have
                 my head buttered. Goodbye. Happy meeting you.
                 (Exits.)

ROGER   His head buttered? I think it's soft enough already.

BOO-BOO   But he didn't mention anything about leopards and
                 tigers.

TASKLEY   (Putting head back round kitchen door.) Watch
                 out for the leopards and tigers. Can't have any-
                 thing happen to you both now! (Exits.)

ROGER   He is mad.

TIM   Thanks a lot, folks. One day I might tell you how
                 much you've helped.

ROGER   You know, I didn't read that before I signed it. I
                 hope I'm not due for ten years in the Foreign
                 Legion.

BOO-BOO   I'm safe enough. My contract was for a beauty
                 column which I suspect you are going to write.

TIM   And very well it's going to pay too.

BOO-BOO   Even as Primrose Lane I always read anything
                 before I sign it.

TIM	Really. (Produces paper form from envelope in pocket.) In that case I take it that you are willing to pose for nude photographs.
ROGER	She most certainly is not.
TIM	Relax, I'm kidding. But when I let her practise her signature that is what it said on the paper.
BOO-BOO	It did not. I read it. It was something about horoscopes.
TIM	It wasn't you know. (Looks at paper.) Bloody hell, it was too! You know what's happened, don't you?
KATIE	No.
TIM	I've given Myrtle the wrong one. She'll think Taskley's asked her to appear starkers in 'Flesh-pot'.
KATIE	You steaming idiot. What's going to happen now?
ROGER	Sorry, but Boo-Boo and I can't wait to find out. We've got some arrangements to make for the wedding.
BOO-BOO	Are we going to a wedding?
ROGER	Not going to one - having one.
BOO-BOO	You mean....? Oh Roger! (They embrace.)
KATIE	Congratulations. (Nudges TIM who is deep in thought.) Tim!
TIM	Oh, yes. All the best.
ROGER	Let's get your things. Where are they?
BOO-BOO	Upstairs.

(ROGER and BOO-BOO start to mount the stairs.)

Mrs Weston-Lamb. I've always wanted to be double-barrelled.

ROGER   I promise you will be.

(ROGER and BOO-BOO exit upstairs.)

KATIE   Things happen so fast round here.

TIM   I'll say. How are we going to pacify Gypsy Rose Lee out there?

(MYRTLE comes out of caravan.)

My God, here she comes!

KATIE   You'll just have to say that it was all your fault - that you gave her the wrong contract.

TIM   If she's still talking to anybody. Imagine asking her to pose for nude photographs.

(MYRTLE enters french windows.)

Miss Boggsley, about that letter I gave you from Mr Taskley.

MYRTLE   I can't divulge the contents as I have not yet given Mr Taskley my answer, but I am sure you can see how radiantly happy it has made me.

KATIE   It has?

MYRTLE   To tell the truth, I've never seen anything in myself to admire. I've never really attracted men - and now this proposal out of the blue.

TIM   Are you sure you know what you'll be taking on - I mean taking off?

KATIE   Tim, leave this to me. I think, Myrtle, you may

not have understood the full implications of Mr
Taskley's offer. You do realise that for at least
some of the time you will have to be completely
naked?

MYRTLE   Why should that worry me? I'll be married before
              then.

TIM   You're getting married?

KATIE   Will your husband agree to photographs?

MYRTLE   Of course. I expect he'll want lots to send to his
              relatives.

TIM   His relatives!

MYRTLE   Naturally. After all, he'll be in the photographs
              as well.

KATIE   It gets worse.

MYRTLE   Before another minute passes, there's something
              I'd like to get off my chest.

TIM   Don't trouble. I'll buy the magazine.

MYRTLE   You'll buy the magazine? That's wonderful.
              Aunt Ada's Journal is saved.

KATIE   What has Aunt Ada's Journal got to do with it?

MYRTLE   That's what I'm trying to tell you, only it's rather
              difficult as I'm not exactly proud of what I've done.
              I didn't merely happen to stop here for accommo-
              dation. I came to the village on purpose. I
              wanted to sign up your writers for my magazine.

TIM   Your magazine?

MYRTLE   Aunt Ada's Journal. My friend Edith suggested
              it, actually. She thought that if I managed to sign
              up some of the Village Almanac contributors I'd

be able to take things a little easier. You see -
promise you won't breathe a word - I write it all
myself.

KATIE   Join the club. (She collapses into helpless laugh-
                        ter.)

MYRTLE   You mean he writes the whole of Village Almanac?

                        (KATIE nods.)

TIM   You picked a hell of a time to come out with that
                        announcement.

MYRTLE   But what about all the people I met - Adam,
                        Primrose Lane. And however do you manage?
                        It's eight pages thicker than mine, and that takes
                        so much time I'm making no progress with the
                        recipe book I'm trying to write.

TIM   (Dejectedly.) That's the secret out, then. So much
                        for my rosy literary future.

KATIE   Tim, I'm sorry. I didn't think. Somehow it just
                        seemed so funny.

TIM   Well, now you can laugh all the way to the Labour
                        Exchange.

MYRTLE   Please don't be upset. I know far too much about
                        the problems of producing a magazine solo to
                        breathe a word. As far as I'm concerned, I've
                        forgotten the whole thing already.

TIM   You really mean that?

MYRTLE   Your secret is safe, I promise. The main thing
                        is you've said you'll buy Aunt Ada's Journal. I'd
                        have been so sorry to see it discontinue publica-
                        tion. The old ladies love it so.

TIM   (Aghast.) Buy Aunt Ada's Journal? Just a
                        minute.........

MYRTLE   It's such a relief. I'm going to be so busy with
                wedding plans.

                (ROGER and BOO-BOO start to come downstairs
                with case.)

KATIE   (to MYRTLE) When is your wedding?

ROGER   Four weeks on Saturday.

TIM   Oh, that wedding.

BOO-BOO   I'm so happy I could kiss everybody.

TIM   You may.

                (BOO-BOO kisses TIM.)

KATIE   What would you like for a wedding present?

ROGER   Leave it up to you, but we'd prefer something solid
                gold.

TIM   Solid gold? That's a promise.

BOO-BOO   Roger?

ROGER   Yes, darling?

BOO-BOO   Will I be able to have a white wedding?

ROGER   Only if it snows! Goodbye.

BOO-BOO   Bye!

                (ROGER and BOO-BOO exit front door.)

KATIE   I think we could use a drink. Myrtle?

MYRTLE   Perhaps on this occasion, just a tiny one. I'm not
                really used to alcohol.

TIM   I hope it doesn't loosen your tongue.

MYRTLE

Rely on me. I shall keep as tight as a newt. I think that's the expression.

TIM

You're a good sport, Myrtle.

(TIM pours drinks as TASKLEY enters from the kitchen.)

TASKLEY

I have something to say to you all. Today I made a very important decision.

MYRTLE

The answer's yes, Mr Taskley. Yes, yes, yes.

TASKLEY

I'm getting married.

TIM

It's an epidemic.

TASKLEY

(Moving close to MYRTLE.) I came here looking for someone to help out with my future and I have found her. Little did I think that the same person would consent to be my wife.

MYRTLE

(Simpering.) It was preordained. My prognostications were correct.

TASKLEY

Good. In that case I shouldn't need to tell you that I don't require your professional services.

MYRTLE

You don't like working wives. I understand.

TASKLEY

When the future Mrs Taskley leaves here with me, her working days are over. (Opens kitchen door and calls:) I've told them, darling. Come and be congratulated.

TIM

You don't mean.......?

(MRS -ER enters shyly from the kitchen.)

TASKLEY

Meet my fiancée.

(Blank astonishment on the faces of TIM, KATIE and MYRTLE.)

MRS -ER   No wonder you're surprised. I am myself. Never
                       thought I'd be stepping down the aisle to 'Here
                       comes the -er.'

MYRTLE   (Babbling incoherently.) But I thought....... I
                       mean surely..... There must be some ....

TIM   I don't understand. You said you had found some-
                       body who could help your future.

TASKLEY   She's done that already, though not in the way I
                       expected. Though she doesn't know it, this
                       charmer is an accomplished phrenologist.

KATIE   Phrenologist? What's that?

TASKLEY   Bumps. She reads cranial bumps. When she was
                       putting the butter on my head she gave me an
                       extremely accurate character reading.

TIM   She did?

TASKLEY   She said I was easily taken in.

KATIE   Surely not, Mr Taskley.

TASKLEY   Oh yes, Katie, that has been true in the past, but
                       this perceptive lady has made me realise that
                       knowledge of one's own character is more val-
                       uable than all the horoscopes in the world.

TIM   It's a point of view.

TASKLEY   Out there in the kitchen I saw that I was capable
                       of making my own decisions, and to celebrate I
                       made a very important one and asked her to
                       marry me.

MRS -ER   And I said I -er.

                       (Wail from MYRTLE who sinks on to nearest
                       seat.)

KATIE   (Uneasily.) That's wonderful. Well, Mrs -Er,

I hope you'll be very happy in the new life ahead
of you. (Meaningfully.) I expect you'll completely
forget about all that's happened here in the village.

MRS -ER   (to KATIE) I know which side my bread's -er.

TASKLEY   What's that about bread, darling?

TIM   She hopes we won't miss her sandwiches too much.
                 She makes lovely sandwiches.

TASKLEY   I'm looking forward to some real English home
                 cooking. Well now, Tim, when is it safe for us
                 to leave?

TIM   Any time you like. I got the O.K. a few minutes
                 ago.

TASKLEY   That's swell.

TIM   Mr Taskley, we're still waiting to hear. What
                 have you decided to do about the magazine?

TASKLEY   I intend to keep both plants going in the meantime.
                 Your syndicated columns will give 'Home Spun' a
                 new lease of life, so I reckon it can carry Task-
                 ley's Tinted Tissues for a spell.

TIM   Is that wise? I thought you said the tissue market
                 had hit bottom.

TASKLEY   Tissues had what?

TIM   Hit bottom.

TASKLEY   Tim, you're brilliant. That's it. From now on
                 it's going to be Taskley's Tinted Toilet Tissue!

KATIE   Toilet Tissue? Will you sell more that way?

TASKLEY   More than anyone else. I've just had a humdinger
                 of an idea. I'll print a horoscope on every twelfth
                 sheet and if that doesn't increase consumption,

I don't know what will.

TIM   Incredible.

TASKLEY   Well, goodbye folks, and thanks a lot for every-
                        thing. Come along, Marigold.

                        (TASKLEY and MRS -ER exit front door.)

TIM   }
KATIE   }   (Laughing.) Marigold!

                        (Laughter stops as they see MYRTLE sitting
                        dejectedly.)

KATIE   Myrtle, I'm so sorry.

TIM   So am I, but whatever made you think.......

MYRTLE   The letter. The letter he gave me. (She produces
                        letter and reads.)
                        'Just moments after meeting you I felt that fate
                                                             was kind,
                        I knew at once quite suddenly our hearts had
                                                             entwined,
                        For years I've searched for such as you with
                                                    whom to share my life,
                        My darling, how I love you - please consent to
                                                             be my wife. '

                        (MYRTLE, in tears, rushes to french windows,
                        then turns, her misery changing to anger.)

                        Horoscopes on toilet paper, indeed! I hope he
                        gets a Scorpio in his Uranus!

                        (MYRTLE rushes into caravan and slams door.)

TIM   Poor old thing. I hope she gets over it.

KATIE   Why don't you buy 'Aunt Ada's Journal' from her
                        and give her more time for her cookery book?
                        She'd still probably do the odd article for you,

and that way you'd get on faster with your thriller.

TIM
And where am I going to get the cash to....? Of course - with Taskley's money I suppose I could now.

KATIE
Exactly. Amalgamate the magazines and you'd double the number of readers.

TIM
I think I'll have to get Myrtle to do the next episode of the serial.

KATIE
Why?

TIM
The last is going to be rather difficult to follow. You remember it ended with the Vicar slipping a note through the letter-box of Violet Brown, the timid church organist?

KATIE
So?

TIM
I've just realised that it reads, '£1000 for your nude photograph in my magazine'.

KATIE
That should make the old ladies' bedsocks tingle.

TIM
Hey, we never did have those drinks.

(TIM fetches drinks.)

KATIE
We're going to need all the money we can get. Did I hear you promise Roger and Boo-Boo a wedding present of solid gold? What did you have in mind?

TIM
A load of manure.

(TIM gives KATIE a drink and puts his arm round her.)

Well, here's to ...... What?

KATIE
Let's see. 'Aunt Ada's Homespun Village

Almanac Journal'?

(They clink glasses and drink. There is a pause
as both separately muse over the recent happen-
ings.)

TIM   Been a funny kind of day.

CURTAIN

<u>FURNITURE AND PROPERTY LIST</u>

<u>ACT I</u>

On Stage:

Settee	on it: 3 cushions
Armchair	on it: 1 cushion
Small chair	
Desk chair	
Desk	on it: Typewriter, ruler, eraser, typed manuscript of magazine, jar with pencils and pens, white envelopes, typing paper, sheet of paper with poem typed on it, 'Village Almanac', thick felt marker, 2 short lengths of string, sheets of blank paper, small tray with teapot, sugar, milk, cup, saucer and teaspoon.
	In drawer: Large brown envelopes, stamps.
Dresser	on it: Vase containing folded slips of paper, cow bell, vase for flowers, assorted pottery and brass objects.
Small table	on it: 1 bottle gin, 1 bottle brandy, 1 bottle whisky, 6 glasses, 2 bottles ginger ale, 2 bottles tonic.
Small table (R) on it:	Potted plant.
Window sill	on it: Indoor watering-can with water, potted plants.
Stereo	on it: Demonstration record and sleeve.
Tiger skin rug	
Wall	on it: Gun (above stereo)
	Calendar (below landing)
	Bellows, horse brasses and small pictures
Garden bench	

Doors and hatch closed, french windows open.

Off Stage:

Off Garden: Basket with aerosol spray, gardening gloves, bunch of flowers (KATIE)

Off Upstairs: Astrology books (TIM)

Off Kitchen: Basket of cleaning materials, including duster (KATIE)
4 sandwiches, each larger and more unattractive than the previous (MRS -ER)
1 presentable sandwich (KATIE)
Plate for sandwiches

Off Cupboard:	Old-fashioned telephone
Off Front Door:	2 suitcases (MYRTLE) 1 suitcase (BOO-BOO) Matching make-up case (BOO-BOO) In it: lipstick, perfume, eyebrow pencil, jars, bottles 'Fleshpot' and 'Homespun' magazines (TASKLEY) Briefcase (TASKLEY) In it: 3 contracts, 3 small,printed forms
PERSONAL:	ROGER - Diary, pen, monogrammed handkerchief TIM - Handkerchief TASKLEY - Wallet, Newspaper clipping, £10

ACT II

On Stage:

As Act I,with Tigerskin rug in lifelike position on bench,facing caravan door.

Off Stage:

Off Kitchen:	Plastic bowl of egg-white (shaving lather) spatula and towel (KATIE) Blue overall (KATIE) Cup of coffee (KATIE)
Off upstairs:	Black 'doctor's' bag (BOO-BOO) In it: wall thermometer
PERSONAL:	ROGER - £10 TIM - Car keys

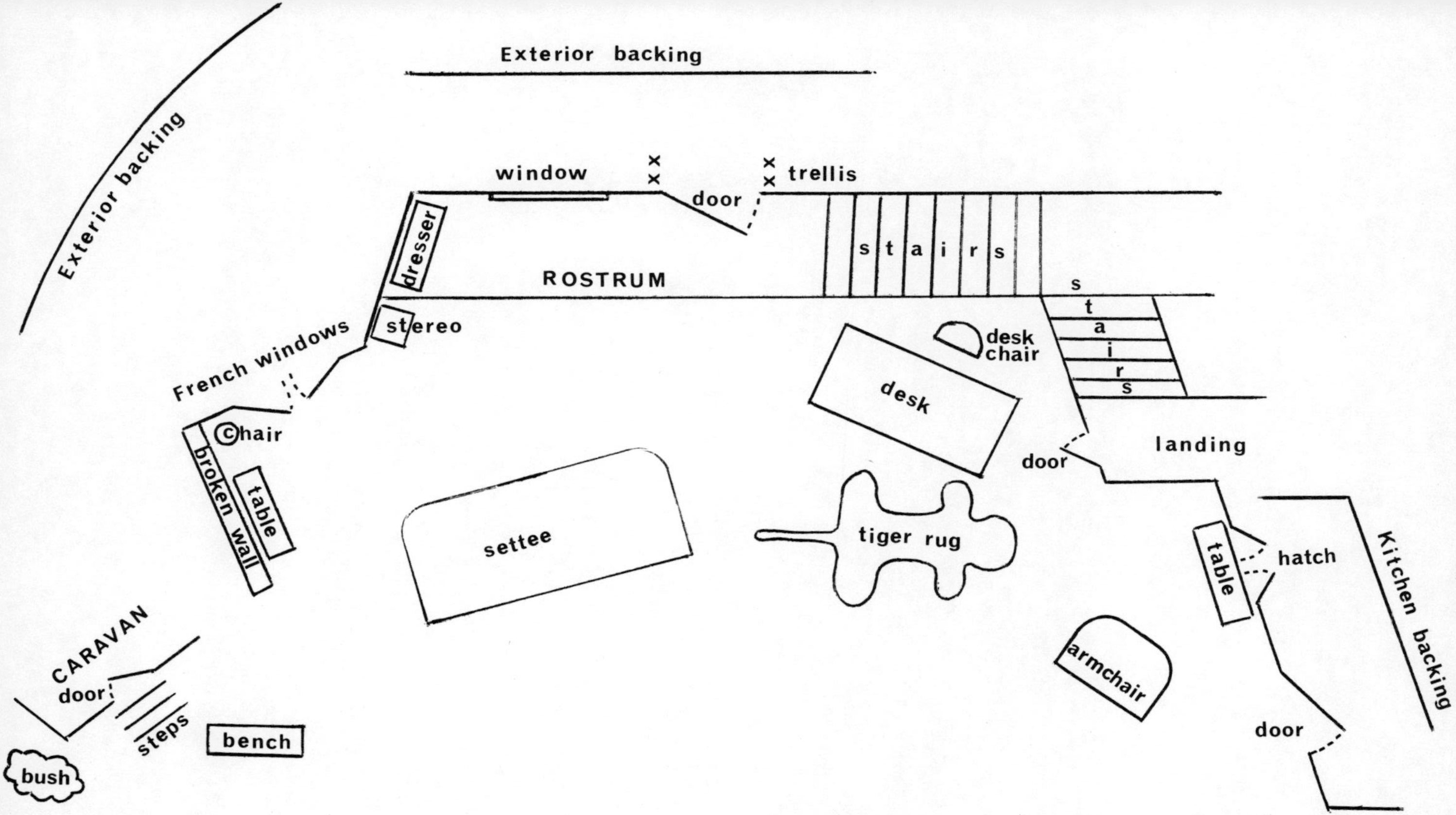

Exterior backing
Exterior backing
window
door
trellis
dresser
ROSTRUM
stairs
stairs
stereo
desk chair
French windows
desk
chair
landing
door
broken wall
table
settee
tiger rug
table
hatch
Kitchen backing
CARAVAN
door
armchair
steps
bench
door
bush